Jessica Hatzis and Bree Johnson are the co-founders of the cult beauty brand frank body and the branding agency Willow & Blake. Copywriters and brand builders by trade, they are passionate about teaching the next generation of entrepreneurs to create their own successful businesses from scratch.

FROM THE GROUND UP

Jessica Hatzis + Bree Johnson

affirm press

affirm press

First published in Australia in 2026 by Affirm Press,
a Simon & Schuster (Australia) Pty Limited company
Wurundjeri Woiwurrung Country
Level 3, 162 Collins Street, Melbourne VIC 3000

Affirm Press is located on the unceded land of the Wurundjeri Woiwurrung peoples of the Kulin Nation. Affirm Press pays respect to their Elders past and present.

New York Amsterdam/Antwerp London Toronto Sydney/Melbourne New Delhi
Visit our website at www.simonandschuster.com.au

AFFIRM PRESS and design are trademarks of Affirm Press Pty Ltd, Inc., used under licence by Simon & Schuster, LLC.

10 9 8 7 6 5 4 3 2 1

NATIONAL LIBRARY OF AUSTRALIA

A catalogue record for this book is available from the National Library of Australia

9781923293953 (paperback)
9781761822551 (ebook)

Cover design by Alissa Dinallo
All internal diagrams and tables © Jessica Hatzis and Bree Johnson
Typeset by Post Pre-press Group in 12/17 pt Garamond Premier Pro
Printed and bound in Australia by the Opus Group

FSC www.fsc.org MIX Paper from responsible sources FSC® C001695

To the next generation of entrepreneurs. A rising tide lifts all boats.

CONTENTS

PROLOGUE

It was 9pm on a wintery Melbourne evening in June of 2012. We were sitting in our very cold, very dark office (a term we used loosely for the building we inhabited). Sure, it had walls and doors; mostly. One of them opened up to a sheer drop from the second floor into a concrete car park below.

But heating? No.

A kitchen? Only if you ventured into the apartment next door.

Wi-fi? Thank god for tethering.

Willow & Blake was only 18 months old at this point, and we were still scraping by from pay cheque to pay cheque and pouring every ounce of ourselves into our work.

The deadline was looming on a tone of voice document for a leading financial institution that another advertising agency had outsourced to us at the last minute. The project would usually take a large, experienced team a few weeks to complete, but here we were – three relatively young writers with 48 hours to pull it together; our reputations and bellies on the line. We needed this project to come off without a hitch. We had been working around the clock for the last month for another client who, despite being on the *Australian Financial Review Rich List* for the fifth year running, was dodging all calls and emails related to his unpaid bills.

We were running out of money. Fast.

*

There it was – 10 feet high and 30 feet wide.

Our little coffee scrub had been blown up to gigantic proportions and plastered across the front windows of MECCA stores all over Australia.

Two writers stood humbled: one on a pedestrian crossing on Little Lonsdale Street as the traffic flew past dangerously close to her; the other inside the gargantuan walls of Highpoint, the smell of donuts and noodles lingering in the air.

Both of us were pinching ourselves that we had actually pulled this off.

How, in just four years, did we get here?

Chapter 1

SOME PEOPLE C*NT SPELL – WE CAN

No one becomes a writer hoping to get rich quick. So how did two twenty-somethings armed with nothing but their laptops, a lifetime supply of Red Bull and their words become responsible for building over a billion dollars' worth of brands?

It's a good question – one that people seem interested in knowing the answer to. So we thought we'd do what we do best and write it down.

You've probably heard of the skincare brand that we launched in 2013 – frank body.

You may not have heard of our branding agency, Willow & Blake, but we're sure you've heard of some of our clients: DISSH, July, Briogeo, Bondi Sands and KEVIN.MURPHY, to name a few.

Building a brand is an art – one rooted in intuition and science, where insight-led strategies are the key to unlocking huge growth potential and a community of raving fans. In this book we want to take you through our process – a repeatable process – for building brands that people love.

This isn't your standard marketing textbook. No one needs another dry read written from the nosebleed heights of an ivory tower.

Pour yourself your drink of choice and get comfortable. To understand where we are today, as experts in our field with 40 combined years of brand-building experience, we need to take you back to where it all began.

Before we go any further, it's important to introduce you to the other co-founders of Willow & Blake and frank body. This period of our lives was very much like the sitcom *Friends*. Think five twenty-somethings living together, working together, dancing around a sofa.

First, we have Bree and Jessica, who are writing this book. You'll learn more about us in the pages that follow.

Next, Erika Geraerts. Erika is also the co-founder of Willow & Blake. She exited both companies in 2016. For years, Jess, Bree and Erika were inseparable. We all worked together at Red Bull and went through a debaucherous period living together and/or across the road from each other. We called ourselves 'The Tripod' or 'The Vagina Club'. Like Jess and Bree, Erika is a copywriter by trade, a deep thinker and a brilliant creative. She went on to found another beauty brand called Fluff.

The second is Alex Boffa. The only founder with relevant education when it comes to starting a business, Alex studied entrepreneurship at RMIT while simultaneously founding and running global record label Chameleon Recordings. He went on to be Head Agent at 360 music agency, which is where he and Jess met. Spoiler alert: Alex became frank body's Chief Operating Officer (COO) and was responsible for spearheading frank body's global operations, ensuring we had localised distribution in the United States (US) and United Kingdom (UK) a year after launching. You'll hear from him later as a subject matter expert in operations.

And finally, Steve Rowley. When Steve is asked to list his profession, he simply writes: 'business'. Because to explain what he does would take too much time and, as we know, time is money. After bailing out of a horticulture degree, Steve took ownership of a small cafe and bar. He grew that into Sixty-One Group, a hospitality group responsible for over $20 million annual revenue and more than 200 staff. He and Bree met in 2019 the 'old-fashioned way': at a bar after too many espresso martinis. She saved him in her phone as 'blue shirt guy'. They are now married with two children. He made the very first batch of frank by hand and went on to become frank body's Chief Executive Office (CEO).

When we met, we were all in the early stages of our careers; ambitious, broke and drawn together by a common desire to live a life less ordinary – or, as a starting point, a life where we could afford our rent.

We had a healthy appetite for risk, a get-shit-done attitude and enough tenacity to give it a real crack.

*

The year was 2010.

Kesha's song 'TiK ToK' had stayed atop the Hot 100 for nine weeks. Our love for the written word (and memes) was as strong as our commitment to Dream Matte Mousse and Sally Hansen's Airbrush Legs.

While our friends were out doing what most twenty-somethings did at the time, we were doing something a bit different.

We lived together in an apartment in Melbourne's bayside suburb of Elwood, and most days and nights you would find us sprawled across the faded pink sofa, each with our chunky white (not silver) MacBooks, clacking away at the keys. Jess wrote about music, Bree wrote about fashion and beauty and Eri wrote about food. Ah yes, the days of WordPress blogs were golden.

We'd all been told that writing wasn't a viable career.

'Eighty per cent of journalism graduates won't get a job in journalism' – this was from the Head of Journalism at Monash University, said to Bree on the first day of her journalism degree. Inspiring.

'There are no jobs in writing. Why don't you do your career project on being in the army?' – this was from Jess's high school career counsellor, who neglected to notice the fact that Jess had not so much as a demerit point on her record and hated confrontation. Not exactly the ideal candidate for weaponised battle.

And yet, we had a dream to combine our blogs into one online magazine where we could write our little hearts out.

There was one rather large problem, however. We were broke. We'd moved out of home in our very early twenties and alongside studying full time, we also worked multiple part-time jobs to pay the bills. Between the rent on our apartment and our addiction to avocado and goat's cheese toast, there wasn't much left over at the end of the week. Somehow, we always managed to pay our internet bill, potentially because access to our blogs was considered essential in our household.

Writing certainly didn't pay the bills, but one fateful day it did earn us our first break. The divine word gods smiled on us when our co-founder Erika spotted a competition that would mean, if we won, we would have a website made for us, saving us what was estimated to be about $10,000 at the time. All we had to do was explain our concept in 150 words or less. Hold our toast.

We won that competition and Willow & Blake (W&B) the digital magazine was born.

Next, we had to decide what we wanted to write about. We decided not to go down the well-worn path of fashion, music and food but instead focus on people; people we didn't know, but who inspired us. People who were in our lives and, sometimes, people we made up. We always say that if we were to start W&B today it would probably be a podcast. We're glad it wasn't, as we much prefer being behind our laptops than in front of cameras or microphones.

Our style might've been considered unorthodox. We didn't conduct formal interviews. Instead, we would meet our interviewees at a place where they felt comfortable – their house, a local cafe, a bar or restaurant – and we would chat, often for multiple hours.

The informal nature allowed us to really get to know the person.

We'd then go away and write a profile of them. Not a polished, carefully constructed interview, but a piece that showed them how we saw them in all their beautiful rawness. Some people didn't like how honest we were – never offensive (hopefully), but observant and deducing. However, our readers loved it.

Our following grew quickly, bolstered by our dedication to finding, creating and posting memes daily on Facebook. Yes, you read that correctly: Facebook.

Willow & Blake started to take on a life of its own, growing into something bigger than a blog. We started throwing parties that attracted hundreds of people trying to get an invite, bringing together a crowd of Melbourne's aspiring artists, writers, entrepreneurs and those seeking a free espresso martini – the drink du jour in 2009.

While this was happening, we each graduated uni, said goodbye to our jobs at Red Bull (and the denim short-shorts we had become accustomed to wearing as part of our uniform) and ventured out into the real world to secure our first big girl jobs. Pants required.

Jess nabbed a role as Head of Public Relations (PR) and Content at 360 Agency, a job that had come about entirely as the result of her music blog 'Who is Amelie'. Yes, she had a lot of blogs going on at the time.

Although she was a writer through and through, music had always been an important part of Jess's life. Jess loved reviewing gigs and albums, and before long the blog gained unexpected traction among fellow music nerds. The music agency that ended up hiring her straight out of university (she actually interrupted her master's degree studies to take the job) was looking for an all-rounder to handle everything from travel logistics to PR and copywriting for their music agency and their new PR arm that repped brands all over Australia. They saw Jess's writing and liked it. She was up for anything and knew that she'd regret not taking the opportunity far more than putting her thesis on hold – she knew she could always go back to uni if she needed to. Taking that job was one of the best decisions she ever made. Her master's degree is still waiting patiently for her to return.

Meanwhile, Bree had worked her way up from intern to Acting Editor at cult publication *Broadsheet*, one latte at a time.

Reading that Mia Freedman had become the editor of *Cosmopolitan* by the age of twenty-four, Bree had decided that was a good goal. She did her internships at the glossy magazines up in Sydney (*Cleo* and *Girlfriend*), but realised quickly they weren't for her. Instead, she nabbed an internship at a new Melbourne-based publication called *Broadsheet*. There, Bree met her boss, who became her mentor. She saw what he was building and wanted to be part of it. Asking to do extra days (for free), Bree took on more responsibilities, upskilled herself with an editing course and eventually built up the courage to ask for a job. Starting as Editorial Assistant and their third in-house employee, she quickly worked her way up to Acting Editor at age twenty-five before deciding that was close enough to tick that life goal off her list. Bree learned a lot at *Broadsheet*, including when to listen and when to talk, the importance of hard work and hustle, where the best eggs are in Melbourne, and also that she didn't want to work for an entrepreneur – she wanted to be one.

After almost two years of writing Willow & Blake (the blog), ideas started to rumble for Willow & Blake (the business). We were working in great jobs under the leadership of wonderful entrepreneurs, and we could now see ourselves becoming entrepreneurs ourselves. This coincided nicely with the freelance copywriting requests that started to come in from friends – a pleasant twist in our story that we didn't see coming.

Until this point, in our experience as copywriters, most clients treated words as an afterthought – forced to squish, bend and conform to the needs of the brand's visual design, rather than working in tandem or even being the main focus, as we knew they should. This is when we first saw a gap in the market: there was an opportunity to start an agency that built brands with words and messaging at their core. Freelance copywriters were aplenty, but an agency that specialised in copy? That didn't exist as far as we could tell. An eyebrow was raised. A discussion was had. A scribble was drawn on a napkin at a bar after one too many nightcaps. We knew what we needed to do. We quit our jobs and launched our agency.

There we were, capable of delivering wit with the sharpness of a surgical blade – but we had a lot to learn when it came to the realities of running a business. On our very first day, Jess and Erika walked downstairs in their sharehouse, wearing PJs, looked at each other and said, 'Right, so how do we actually do this?'

What followed was not work, but a long sunbaking session on the rooftop of our house, where we contemplated the merits of a partnership versus a company, not really understanding the true meaning of either. The meeting concluded with Erika accidentally locking Jess on the roof for several hours.

Things were off to a flying start.

Over the coming months, Willow & Blake was formed based on a series of guiding principles:

- Be kind and curious
- Be patient and persistent
- Understand that sometimes a blue curtain is just that
- Accept that differences make us who we are.

But more about those later.

We were finding our feet in the world of small business by emailing everyone we knew. The subject line: *Coffeewriting – what is that?*

We were sending out our pitch and folio in a nutshell, a subject line designed to pique people's interest in a sea of emails with subject lines like 'Hello' and 're: ....'. We showed from the very moment people engaged with us that we could do things differently, in a way that could catch their attention without having to try too hard.

Some responses were great, and some were horrible. The misogyny entrenched deeply in our industry reared its ugly head early on. Despite being in our mid-twenties at this point, we were called 'girls' a lot – something we had not been for a decade. Our age was pointed out alongside comments about our lack of knowledge on subjects that our male counterparts of the same age must have been born with. Lucky them. We forged on. We established a value system early on that meant we didn't lament losing those jobs – instead, we were thankful we didn't end up working with people who held narrow and outdated views. We were determined to make it in an industry of people who didn't move through the world in the way we did. We knew we had a unique view to offer and it was one that was desperately needed.

We had taken a leap from our low-paying jobs into our own business, which paid even less. We were young and naive, but also enthusiastic and fuelled by coffee: a winning combination, if you ask us. We loved every minute of it and if we're being honest – no one becomes a writer to make money.

Finally, someone responded with a work opportunity. Little did we know, it would be the beginning of a project that would change Willow & Blake forever.

THE LESSON:

If you never ask, the answer will always be no.

Chapter 2

WHAT IS A BRAND AND WHY DOES IT MATTER?

Our big break started with a pallet of 20,000 plastic shoes.

There we were, surrounded by a small sample: dozens of red, blue and clear plastic strappy sandals. Our feet poured in and out of each one, stomping up and down stairs, laneways and curbs. Those shoes were held up in the air next to ivy walls, dangled off couches and from buildings. We didn't just talk the talk – when it came to our first big project, we literally walked the walk.

Do you remember jelly sandals? They are the plastic shoes you might have had as a child. Perfect for muddy puddles, spills and whatever adventures little feet get up to. Our client and friend had ordered 20,000 adult-sized jelly sandals. His thought was that teenagers and young adults would also like a little adventure in their life. Our job was to convince them.

He gave us full creative license to take the business and build it into a brand.

We got to work with a brand and social strategy.

The opportunity for this brand was clear; the product was unique already. We had a niche audience of teenagers and young adults who would remember the product from their childhood and so we decided to build their brand story around adventure and nostalgia.

Our key tactic was based on our target demographic. The pervasive fear of missing out (FOMO) experienced by this audience meant that social proof was key. Get enough of the right people wearing Jelly Beans (that's how we branded them) and the rest of the teenagers would flock like sheep driven by a deep fear of being left out. It was 2013 and all people posted on Instagram were sepia-toned images of their feet and photos of their breakfast, so the content came easily.

We came up with the tagline 'Are you jeally?' and coupled this with a tonne of social proof – think hundreds of feet pics, a bombardment of press, competitions and influencers. And we did it: 10,000 followers on Instagram and 20,000 units sold.

This formed our first noteworthy case study.

From here, Willow & Blake grew quickly, as did our confidence in our ability to build brands.

The hustle was real, but the hard work and long hours we were putting in seven days a week began to grow into larger opportunities that meant we could actually pay our rent and occasionally buy some overpriced avocado on toast. Together, we built a reputation for ourselves as the go-to agency for bold and risky brand ideas that centred around a creative voice and message, often alongside a social or digitally led campaign.

To us, it felt completely organic to look at brands through a digital lens – after all, it was clear that everyone was migrating to social media, so why not take brands along for the ride? We looked at every product through the lens of the potential consumer until we found a unique and easy-to-understand angle that put that customer first. We developed a brand strategy, a tone of voice and a social media plan that was refreshing, distinctive and, of course, built on insight. Funnily enough, the same outdated industry stalwarts who had told us we didn't know what we were doing hadn't thought to try things this way. If you can't join them, beat them.

Despite many successful projects, we also ran into a lot of roadblocks in those early years. These predominantly came from clients who came to us for bold and interesting ideas, but upon seeing those ideas were too scared to take the risk, watering the concept down into something we knew wouldn't work. They didn't understand the importance of brand or believe in our process; they just wanted to know what their return on investment (ROI) would be.

There were many things holding us back, but one kept coming up: fear.

It was a frustrating cycle, as most creatives know, but it was one that raised the question that would change our lives: What if we made our own brand and showed people starting new brands what could be achieved with a unique strategy that you really stuck to?

What many people don't know is that for us, frank body began as a case study. There were no aspirations to make money or grow a global brand, but rather a desire to show our clients what could be achieved if you truly committed to a unique brand identity.

Among the five co-founders of frank body, there was a goal to build a product-based business at the intersection of social media, ecommerce and the growing interest in wellness. Instagram had just launched and was only populated by individuals, not brands. Shopify was a way we could create and launch a business without huge overheads and cumbersome retail timelines. The wellness space was booming.

We explored many different options, from recipe e-books to coconut vodka to light boxes – but none stuck. Note: rancid coconut vodka is not something you want litres of in your house.

Then one day, two ladies came into Steve's cafe in South Melbourne, Station Street Trading Co. It was a small heritage building converted into a bustling cafe.

Most days, Steve stood behind the coffee machine, forever studying the ebb and flow of the room as he drew caramel ribbons of coffee and coaxed milk into soft, silken waves. His hands moved by instinct, letting his mind make silent calculations, and his eyes caught the details others often missed.

Two ladies asked Steve if they could take home a bag of the used coffee grinds. It wasn't an uncommon request, as many people scattered the grounds through their gardens, feeding roots and urging life from the soil. But these women weren't growing roses. They were seeking renewal of a different kind.

They told Steve they were using it at home as a body exfoliator to target skin concerns like cellulite. It was one of those recipes passed down through generations, like chicken soup made to cure a cold. Steve, a true entrepreneur, felt something click inside his head.

Steve spent the rest of his shift mentally mapping out this coffee scrub idea. It ticked all the boxes of what we'd been looking for – a product in the wellness category that could be sold through ecommerce and marketed across social media, targeting women interested in health and beauty.

Steve came home elated and proceeded to download his thoughts. In the eight hours since he'd spoken to the ladies in his store, he had already evolved and improved the product. A quick google had revealed caffeine as the key active ingredient. Hot water extracts the caffeine, so used coffee grinds are basically decaffeinated. He replaced used grinds for freshly roasted beans. And instead of using standard arabica coffee, he had decided to use fresh robusta beans, which are not great for drinking but they are known for their higher caffeine content and lower cost.

Steve also decided to add extra ingredients like natural oils with added skincare benefits and additional natural exfoliators.

Steve's energy was contagious. Bree was curious but also sceptical – surely there was already someone doing this.

We looked online and in stores. There were lots of DIY recipes for coffee scrubs, but no one was manufacturing and selling them at scale. The rest of the exfoliator category was dominated by gentle sugar scrubs or full of synthetic ingredients like microbeads.

Some time later, Steve made the first test batch. He started downstairs at the coffee machine, grinding batch after batch to find the perfect coarseness for exfoliation – not scratchy, but not too soft.

Next, Steve took to the kitchen, flinging cupboard doors open and pulling out additional ingredients. He settled on sugar and salt; both commonly used natural exfoliators.

Bree rummaged through her bathroom cupboard and produced almond oil (a soothing, deeply nourishing hydrator) and orange essence (an essential ingredient to offset the strong coffee scent).

In true startup fashion, Steve mixed the first batch of coffee scrub on the kitchen table in a big silver bowl with a wooden spoon. The other ingredients were still littering the table.

Bree jumped in the shower with the first bag. Admittedly, the product was somewhat lacking in the aesthetics department – it looked like dirt in a brown paper bag. Luckily, it made up for this in the olfactory department. The mix of coffee and orange combined into a deliciously chocolatey scent reminiscent of Jaffas.

Bree quickly covered herself with the contents of the bag. The texture was more coarse than other scrubs she had used, but not scratchy or irritating. As she stepped out of the shower and felt her skin, two thoughts crossed her mind. First, *My skin feels amazing*. And then, *There's something in this*.

She ran out of the bathroom to make Steve feel her skin. He was already bagging up the contents for the others to try.

The Power of Brand

A brand is more than what you see – it's what you feel

'I just want a logo. I don't need the rest of the stuff.'

This is a line we've heard a lot over the years.

And we get it. When we first started in the world of brand and marketing, we didn't fully understand what a brand was. It was an almost completely neglected subject in our marketing degrees. But fifteen years later, we can tell you with our hands on our hearts that brand is the most important part of building a successful business.

Why? Because people don't buy products, they buy stories.

Before starting Willow & Blake and frank body, we didn't work at big branding or advertising agencies so we didn't have a preconceived idea of what 'brand' was or how it should be created. We've never believed in brand triangles, hexagons, pentagons. We're not big fans of trying to fit a brand into any kind of shape, really.

'What is a brand?' kind of sounds like a trick question marketers might use to make normal folks feel silly about not understanding what a brand is. The opposite is true though – we're all just making it up.

In fact, like most marketing terms, it's subjective, open to debate and its definition continues to evolve. So whatever we write here will likely become irrelevant at some point. But you're here to learn and we're here to give opinions, so let's get into dissecting the question 'What is a brand?' by starting with a quick history lesson.

People often think that 'branding' is a relatively new concept, but really it's been around for a very long time. If you go to the British Museum, you can see a metal brand the Ancient Egyptians used to brand (or burn) their mark onto cattle. It is dated 1500 BC.

The fact that humans have felt the need to brand things for so long only emphasises how important it is. It's fundamental to society.

This concept of branding extended to the US, where ranchers created their own marks to indicate ownership over land and cattle. Think *Yellowstone* but less sexy bare-chested cowboys and more grumpy cows with burnt bottoms. Each brand was simple, unique and easy to identify. These are key traits we still advocate for in the brand marks being created today.

In the 19th century, the term 'brand' again evolved with companies putting their mark and name on products including flour, sugar and beer to indicate its source and, more importantly, its quality.

But it's not until we get to the 20th century that the marketing department comes into the picture. With the growth of mass production and marketing, the term 'brand' explodes, becoming synonymous with not just a company's name or logo but their whole identity – meaning both its reputation and consumer perception.

Ding, ding, ding. Customer perception is key.

But before we get to unpacking what makes a brand, here's a quick recap on what a brand *isn't*.

A brand is not:

- your trademark
- your business name
- your logo
- your visual identity
- your products
- your people.

In reality, your brand *is* the effect all of the above has on people. Put simply, 'brand' is your reputation.

Your brand is what people think and feel when they hear your brand name. It's subjective and fluid because every person's individual perception will be unique, based on a combination of factual and perceived characteristics.

If we say the words 'frank body', you might think: *Coffee* (factual). *Cheeky* (subjective). *Fun* (subjective). But what you're really deciding when you think about those things is: *Is this a brand for me? Is it a brand I want in my bathroom? Does it reflect who I am?*

Brands are like cheat sheets that help people make quick decisions about the products and services they buy.

Which is why we will repeat again that your brand is one of the most important parts of your business.

Let's look at another example:

If you're a twenty-something woman in Australia you will likely have heard of DISSH. When we say the word 'DISSH', you might think: *Minimal* (factual). *Luxe* (subjective). *Popular* (subjective). But what you're really deciding is: *If someone asked me where this top was from, would I be proud to show them the label?*

Start with the 'why' behind the words

When we launched Willow & Blake, we were purely a copywriting and social media agency. However, we have always done more than write copy. There was always a *why* behind our words.

At the start of every project, before any clever quips were made and before any puns were written, we would start with the brand strategy. When we first launched our business, we did this part for free. Oops. Like many starting out, we needed to prove ourselves and we lacked the confidence to charge what we should have.

Our process was intuitive. We started with brand and competitor research. We would deep dive into everything we could find out about the client's brand that would inform the public perception: website, reviews, imagery, press, social media and any offline presence. We then did the same for their competitors. Next, we would plot this information into our presentations. Again and again, we found the same trend emerging:

the brands all looked and sounded like their competitors. Their colours and imagery looked the same. They had no clear point of difference and no unique story. Their copy lacked personality or any kind of narrative. If they used words, they were often dot points of key benefits. Brands were dying in a sea of sameness. It was easy for us to show this visually with page after page of homogenised brands.

Next, we created customer profiles. Again, we didn't take the standard approach of listing generic details like age, salary and sex. We used our understanding of the cultural zeitgeist to create very specific profiles that delved into a customer's wants, needs and desires. We were uniquely positioned to understand the inner thoughts of twenty-somethings in a way no fifty-something marketing manager at a Big 4 company could. This is the reason we hire a diverse range of backgrounds, ages, ethnicities and genders in our businesses wherever we can: life experience matters. At the time of writing, we are in our late thirties and we know this consumer group like the backs of our hands. However, life as carefree twenty-somethings is now a foggy memory in our sleep-deprived, child-dominated minds. So, we hire people who are living it right now. Knowing your limitations and weaknesses is important in business and in life.

Our superpower was and still is in identifying the white space – that is, your point of difference within the existing market. Our insights and recommendations are delivered simply, usually something like 'There is a gap for a brand that sounds and talks like X targeting Y audience profile group.' Then we detail how we can help the business get there and bring the idea to life. This process hasn't changed too much over the years, but at Willow & Blake today we have access to more data. Our superpower has evolved to be interpreting data and applying human insight to it. It's fact and gut instinct coming together.

It sounds simple, but done well it's an art.

A brand is a living thing

When creating a brand, it's important to remember that you can influence it but you'll never fully control it. Gone are the days of conglomerates controlling the market. Your brand is ultimately consumed, and shaped by customers' perceptions – so buckle up and get ready to ride the wave, because your fans will make or break you.

The best way to influence your customer's perception is through consistency. Having values, knowing your values and ensuring everyone on your team lives those values. You must also evolve to be relevant. Brands live and grow. Your job is to make sure your brand stays true to its values.

Marketing is everything and everything is marketing

Every interaction someone has with your brand influences their perception of your brand. Therefore, everything you do is marketing. From the smallest detail, like how customer service signs off their emails, to the biggest advertising campaigns; every detail matters.

It doesn't matter if you have a big budget or no budget; you must start with a consistent message – a message that is repeatable and spreadable. The most valuable marketing channels – word of mouth and earned media – are free. But you need to be consistent and clever to get access to these channels.

We have a saying that we live by at Willow and frank: 'The only thing scarier than a new idea is an old one.'

The best ideas don't come from scrolling social media and regurgitating what other brands are doing. The best ideas come from unexpected places. They grab consumers' attention because they are novel. Don't follow what everyone else is doing and expect it to work. Experiment, test, learn. Don't put all your eggs in one basket. Get comfortable with putting lots of ideas out there; some will fly and some will fall. Test small, win big.

Don't miss any opportunity to connect with your customer. At frank body we think of every communication we have as an opportunity to make our customer smile.

At Willow & Blake it would be easy for us to rinse and repeat strategies and concepts for brands and get them signed off, but we know that the same idea that worked for one client won't work for another. Instead, we develop systems and processes that allow us to find unique ideas for each client – and that's what we'll cover in this book.

THE LESSON:

Risk it for the biscuit.

Chapter 3

KNOWING WHAT YOU STAND FOR: VALUES AND INTUITION

You are the sum of your decisions.

So choose wisely.

Freedom. Flexibility. Home. Creativity. Whatever Jess chooses to spend her time on needs to align with these values – they are the guiding principles of her life. Ultimately, everything she says yes to means saying no to something else. Knowing what she stands for is the key to surviving in business. And in life.

For Bree, it's creativity, connection, autonomy and family. Defining her values is one of the most powerful exercises Bree has done. She revisits them each year, but largely, they have remained unchanged.

An ancient piece of wisdom from the Stoic philosopher Epictetus urges us to 'Know first who you are, and then adorn yourself accordingly'.

What does that mean? Well, Epictetus reminds us that understanding our core values isn't a uniquely modern concept. Rather, it's been essential to human development and decision-making for millennia. The Greeks understood that knowing yourself was the foundation of all wisdom. And in our opinion, despite the world changing drastically since the time of Epictetus almost 2000 years ago, this advice remains steadfastly true.

In business, as in life, you need to know why you are doing things. Why do we decide to take one path rather than another? Hopefully, because that path is aligned to what we want and value. Unfortunately, in the competitive world of consumer brands, it is very easy to lose your way, winding up in a destination you had no intention of going to and compromising who you authentically are all in the name of the next milestone.

Learn this lesson early: Growth is not always good. Unless it's of a personal nature, of course.

Learn this one too: Just because others are doing it, doesn't mean you have to.

Business should be intentional, and the goals of your business should be too. We like to summarise this lesson simply: If it's not a fuck yes, it's a hell no. Not quite as profound as Epictetus, but it does the job.

Business will make you question who you are and what you care about because you have to sacrifice so much, give so much and surrender so much. You need to feel confident that you'll wake up one, five or ten years from now and be comfortable with most of the decisions you made. After all, the public element of building a company is on show for the world to see, so you want to be proud of what they witness.

Jess's value system is based on:

- **HOME:** Her family. Her husband. Her children. Her safe place is full of the people and objects she loves. Home is a place that fosters connection and community, where Jess and her family can make memories.

- **CREATIVITY:** The start. Or simply, the option to start. That is the essence of creativity; not what exists, but what could exist.
- **FREEDOM:** The ability to do what she wants, when she wants. To be herself. To know no limits. The freedom to make decisions without stress or fear. The ability to take a leap and know she'll land on her feet.
- **FLEXIBILITY:** The ability to bend, adapt and shape her life as she wishes and never feel stuck, whether that's with time, resources, energy or money.

For Jess, understanding your values is one of the top pieces of advice she gives to all founders. She knows from her own experience that knowing your values helps keep you on track and fulfilled. Acting in alignment with your values is one of the most critical ways to not only lead a happy life, but to build a successful career. When the going gets tough – which it always does – doing something that is connected to more than aspirations of making money is what will help you get through the hard days.

Bree's value system is based on:

- **CREATIVITY:** Finding creativity in her everyday life. As work becomes more about numbers and strategy, she seeks creative projects (inside and out of work) where she can flex this muscle.
- **AUTONOMY:** She creates the life she leads. She controls what she can and lets the rest go. She voices her opinion and speaks clearly about what she wants for herself.
- **FAMILY:** Bree's number one priority. Being present and purposeful. Not only with her kids but also her husband and extended family.

- **CONNECTION:** Human connection is what life is about. Working as a team to achieve goals, writing words that make a stranger feel something, knowing your neighbour's name.

Bree's earlier years were defined by a belief that hard work equals success. As she got older, she realised that the cliches are true, and it turns out that the joy is in the journey – it's the small everyday moments that matter. As Bree approached the end of her thirties, she redefined her core values – but as her husband reminds her, sticking them on the mirror isn't enough. You have to live with them. The reality is that you will falter. The practice is recognising and course-correcting before you go too far.

Now it's over to you. Grab a notepad and write. Think about what your ideal life looks like and what brings you the most peace, excitement or joy. Look for common themes. Don't rush to complete this exercise. Take your time. Edit. Work on this for days – or even better, weeks.

Need some prompts? We've got you. Maybe words coming to mind are:

- **TRAVEL:** Perhaps this is really about curiosity, exploration and learning.
- **LEGACY:** Maybe it's important to you to leave an impact on the world.
- **SERVING OTHERS:** Are you fulfilled most by helping others?
- **SECURITY:** Financial and physical safety may be paramount to you and linked to your childhood.

Choose words that deeply resonate with your authentic self and principles:

- Accountability
- Adventure
- Ambition
- Authenticity
- Autonomy
- Balance
- Beauty
- Career growth
- Collaboration
- Comfort
- Community
- Confidence
- Connection
- Creativity
- Cultural experiences
- Curiosity
- Exploration
- Family
- Friendship
- Financial freedom
- Fitness
- Freedom
- Fun
- Growth
- Health
- Home
- Independence
- Innovation
- Inspiration
- Integrity
- Investment
- Joy
- Leisure
- Mental health
- Mindfulness
- New experiences
- Personal growth
- Prosperity
- Quality of life
- Relaxation
- Self-care
- Self-development
- Social status
- Spirituality
- Success
- Sustainability
- Travel
- Understanding
- Wanderlust
- Wealth
- Wellness
- Work–life balance
- Worldliness
- Zen

As you explore your core values, you need to be extremely honest with yourself.

Don't write down what you think you're supposed to say. Be truthful with yourself about your core wants, needs and values to get to a real outcome. Don't write down that serving others is a high priority if what you actually value is being rich AF or vice versa. We're all different, and that is the beautiful tapestry of life.

The Brain-Gut Connection in Business

Another commonality between business and life is that your intuition will almost always be right. We are huge advocates for data, but even more so for instinct. The biggest regrets we hold are the situations where we didn't listen to our gut, despite it ringing the alarm bells loud and clear. Ignoring that brain–gut connection costs us time, energy, money and sleep.

The value of intuition is completely dismissed by most of the business world. It's intangible, hard to measure and an innately feminine quality that isn't given credit or consideration in a world dominated by male CEOs, founders and investors.

Cultivating a strong sense of self and learning how to tune into your intuition will serve you well in business. For some it manifests as a literal nagging in the stomach. For others it appears as a nervous system overload. Others still experience a constant and recurring thought. For some unfortunate souls, it presents as insomnia. We've had it all, and we've learned to spot the signs early. We have gotten comfortable with voicing our needs and drawing boundaries. But it wasn't always this way.

There have been certain values we have never wavered on, such as the type of industries you couldn't pay us enough to work in. Hello, tobacco. But as two timid writers in the early days of our careers, even when we were running our own companies, we said yes to certain opportunities when we should have said no. Or we said nothing when we should have said something. Call it an aversion to confrontation, a lack of self-belief, imposter syndrome – whatever the label, we had to get over it fast for our own good. It was time to get clear with ourselves, each other and our team about what we valued. We needed to practise the art of sticking to it – that was the key to healthier business practices and healthier lives.

So right now, as you work on your business plan or work in the business you've created, that nagging feeling you have is one you need to listen to. A product that isn't quite right? An opportunity that seems too good to be true? A team member you need to part ways with? A project that you need to step into or let go of? Do the thing your gut is telling you. The more you delay, the worse the consequences.

We used to say that there are a lot of sharks in the industry, circling founders and their teams, selling them the dream and hoping to profit off their hard work. But we came to realise that's a silly metaphor. Sharks are predictable. The predators that we've spotted are more like snakes – unpredictable and dangerous, ready to rear their heads and strike you when you least expect it.

When exercised like a muscle, your intuition can be one of the largest value creators in your business. When ignored, it can be the difference between success and going bankrupt.

Manifestation – What's That All About?

You've likely heard the word 'maifestation' thrown around a lot in recent years, for better or for worse. We've experienced the power of manifestation firsthand – the truth is, it involves very little sitting around fantasising about a better life and there isn't a vision board in sight. The best and most powerful manifestation comes from our most deep-rooted beliefs about ourselves and what is possible. Tell yourself it won't work out, and it won't. Tell yourself it will, and – coupled with hard work and aligned action – you're much more likely to bring that dream to fruition.

In our experience, manifestation is a combination of self-awareness, self-belief and neuropsychology. You need to build the pathways in your brain to take low self-worth behaviours and limiting beliefs and replace them with new ones that allow you to believe, despite any perceived obstacles, that you are worthy of what you want. You must have this belief to succeed in business. It is absolutely imperative.

Why Founder Alignment is Crucial

After almost two decades of friendship, we've now reached that level where we (read: Bree) says obnoxious things like 'You know that place we went with the bread?' and the other (read: Jess) actually does know the exact restaurant she's talking about, where they had a meal eight years prior. We show up wearing the same clothes to events. We buy the same bags while we're travelling in different countries. We can tell how the other is feeling from the tension they are holding in their face or see through their thinly veiled 'I'm fine' responses. And while our friendship has stretched into many different shapes, one thing remains: it's still going strong. Our longstanding friendship is one of our proudest achievements, because we know that not all friendships last so long.

Researcher and storyteller Brené Brown says, 'Clear is kind'. This was a lesson we learned early. We weren't always clear with one another. We weren't always kind. And this challenged us and our founder relationships. No one can read your mind – not even your best friends. To communicate your values and needs, you first need to know what you want and what your values are. It sounds simple, but a lot of people don't know what is truly important to them.

Honest communication, reciprocated effort and allowing for change have been the three key pillars to our strong friendship and founder partnership. These days, we prioritise talking about our personal values and goals. We know our personal and professional worlds are interlinked and when things shift we all need to be aware. If one of us is yearning for a new challenge, role or a whole new chapter, then we speak about it. Change is scary, but the more we speak about our changing needs and wants, the less scary it becomes.

It's also okay for founders to change their minds and follow different paths. Making sure you talk about what you want for your career and life at the beginning of a business venture is vital. Checking in as the years go on is even more important.

If you're building a business with friends – or even just co-founders – here's what you should be discussing.

Dollars and long-term mission

- What salary can you survive on and what salary do you want to work towards?
- Where do you want to be in five to ten years? Do you want to build a unicorn, create a lifestyle business or make a quick exit?
- What if, in five years' time, the company isn't making enough money to pay you the salary you're aiming for?

Talking about money is awkward. Realistically, the company might not be able to pay you what you want – but being open about what you want is essential.

Roles and how they might change

- Who owns what?
- How will responsibilities shift and evolve as the company grows?
- Are you aiming to step back as an employee?
- If so, will you stay on as a shareholder and board member or exit completely?

In the beginning, we double-handled everything. It wasn't until we started to stay in our own lanes, taking on specific roles, that we took off as a business. It's important to understand that there are different stages of your role.

Equity and preparing for dilution

- What's the ownership split? Make sure it's fair and reflects contributions, risk and commitment.
- Consider future dilution. Are you on the same page about taking outside investment? Think carefully about how much of the pie you give away and what that will mean when you exit.

Ownership is decided at the beginning, before you become successful. Ask for what you want and be prepared to back up why you think it's warranted.

Happiness, values and fulfilment

- What are your values and what's important for you in this stage of your life?
- Are you getting that from your role?

Owning a business is about aligning your day-to-day with your values. The more aligned you can be, the less it will feel like work.

Tips on Working and/or Running a Business with Friends, Refined Over 14+ Years

- Assume positive intent. Your co-founder isn't trying to frustrate you.
- Over-communicate. Speak up about the good, the bad and the ugly. Even your best friend can't read your mind.
- Divide and conquer. Play your role and trust that your co-founder is playing theirs.

- Don't talk about work in front of your other friends. It's boring and rude.
- Friendship first. Always.
- People and goals change.
- Celebrate the wins.
- Sometimes it doesn't work. And that's okay.

THE LESSON:

Your first instinct is often the right one.

Chapter 4

SINGLE ORIGINS: THE FIRST TASTE OF FRANK BODY

To truly understand frank body and the strategy behind the brand, you must understand the era it was born in. Let us transport you back to 2013 – because things that seem obvious or even clichéd now were groundbreaking back then.

We were on the cusp of the social media revolution. The word 'wellness' was not yet implanted in our everyday vernacular like it is today. Instead, it was a burgeoning fringe trend spearheaded by millennials and their smartphone-tapping thumbs. We were children of the eighties and nineties, raised on a diet of paparazzi images that promoted heroin-chic, homogenised beauty standards that all but alienated anyone who wasn't tall, thin, blonde and tanned, and confusingly inaccurate information about what was actually healthy. So of course we were a largely disenfranchised generation looking to find a new way of doing things.

With ever-increasing access to information and emerging 'authorities' (soon to be rebranded as 'key opinion leaders' [KOLs] and then later as 'influencers') who broke ranks from the old guard, we saw social media as a portal to an exotic land of new information.

Also, it was a great way to share photos of our feet, coffee and acai bowls.

Until then, as early-twenty-somethings, we had been subjected to a litany of beauty ads that were confusing and repetitive. These ads showed women washing their faces in bowls of water with their eyes open and smiles that looked as though they were forced wide by coat hangers. There were ads of women crossing the street and stopping traffic as they were cat-called by construction workers. Ads promoting bleach-based acne products featuring models who wouldn't experience a single pimple if they spent a year bathing in beef tallow. Ads that outright shamed women for ageing, promising to wind back the clock, one tiny overpriced metallic jar at a time.

It was the era of digital cameras, makeup-caked faces, muted out lips and desperate attempts to regrow the eyebrows we had zealously over-plucked in the years prior. And then someone dropped an iPhone in our hands and everything changed. Suddenly we could form communities of likeminded people from every corner of the globe. Ideas could gain momentum in an instant, which was insanely satisfying for a group of people who had spent their youth being cut off the dial-up internet and MSN Messenger when Mum needed to call someone. 'iF yOu KnOw yOu kNoW.'

Information could suddenly be accessed anytime, anywhere. But not just any information – totally unverified information. We were now dealing with an onslaught of opinion-based content, totally free from fact-checking. And while we now know the dangers of wielding our opinions like tiny digital swords on unsuspecting victims, at the time, it provided a type of freedom our generation had been craving. To break free of societal norms, to wave goodbye to corporations, to discover niches of society that made us feel good. Every generation has their version of this; ours just happened to occur in the palm of our hands. It was this moment, this shifting of the cultural zeitgeist that provided an opportunity that had never been presented before to the young, hopeful and broke. As far as we could see, it was an opportunity that no one had clued onto yet. There it was: the big white space.

In the summer of January 2013, across three different showers in Melbourne, a group of soon-to-be founders scrubbed and rubbed our way to smoothness with the first sample of our Original Coffee Scrub. We had no idea the brown gritty product that we were holding in our hands, and which was splattered all over our shower screens, would go on to be a global business and household name. The scent was all-consuming – coffee infused with orange oil, reminiscent of a certain fruit-shaped chocolate treat. Little did we know, this smell would permeate every fibre of our beings for the next decade.

In each of our showers, the experience was rather similar: we scooped up handfuls of coffee scrub with our hands and smeared it on legs, arms and stomachs, rubbing the coarse grounds in circles and watching as they rinsed off our bodies and swirled around our feet before eventually finding their way down the drain.

We were no newbies to body scrubs, so we thought we knew what to expect – but as though it has been delivered directly by the beauty gods themselves, this product was different. Our skin had never felt so soft or so smooth; it even looked perkier, instantly. It might've felt absurd to use, but that was part of its charm. We knew at that moment that we had something special. And this little coffee scrub, so different to anything else out there, deserved a brand to match.

After trying the product, it was immediately obvious that everyone was on the same page – we were going to do this.

The Original Coffee Scrub, a six-ingredient body scrub designed to give you extremely soft and smooth skin, would be packed in a humble brown coffee bag – a nod to its hero ingredient and a convenient way to ship product at the time that allowed us to take advantage of large-letter postage costs, saving us a fortune. It would be priced affordably, at $14.95. It would be available only online via frankbody.com – which, in itself, was the commencement of a new shopping behaviour for so many people. It would be marketed primarily through Instagram – a totally new concept for brands and advertising. There were quite literally, as far as we could tell, only a handful of brands on Instagram – all of them small startups from people who saw the same opportunity we did.

So here we were, with something that looked like dirt in a brown paper bag, about to embark on the challenge of convincing people to buy this coffee body scrub instead of the artificial gel-based, fruity-tooty body scrubs full of microbeads that they were used to. Like the product, the brand had to be the antithesis of the beauty industry as we knew it. We'd all been sold enough lies and overpriced products. We couldn't dress this up with bells and whistles – from the six-ingredient formula and handmade practices that got it to your bathroom cupboard, to the issues and ideas that were relevant to a generation of young women, we needed to be honest, transparent and *frank*.

That was the 'aha!' moment that led to 37 million products being sold over the next ten years. And let's be frank – we had no idea what we were getting ourselves into.

THE LESSON:

The only thing scarier than a new idea is an old one.

Chapter 5

HOW TO DEVELOP A CULT BRAND

We had the product, the distribution strategy, the target market and what could loosely be called a marketing plan. Now we needed a brand.

For many years, people have told us we're lucky. And it always makes us pause. The word niggles at us like a slightly crooked picture frame. A common definition of luck is 'success or failure apparently brought about by chance rather than through one's own actions.' Which, in the case of frank body, is incorrect. Yes, a lot went right for us – luck certainly played a role. But behind the success of frank body was a disruptive brand strategy that made things go right.

In the early days of frank body, our strategy wasn't articulated succinctly in a brand document like we would do for our Willow & Blake clients today. It was hastily put together in Google Docs, on butcher's paper, on napkins and in our heads. It wasn't perfected or polished and it evolved as we grew – but it existed and, most importantly, we all knew what it was.

Our process has evolved a lot since those days, but the bones of a good strategy, no matter how it is documented, remain the same.

If you are in the early stages of creating a brand, there's a lot you have to do. Among all the business plans and cash flow forecasts, we're advocates for having a brand strategy. And writing it down. Having a strategy in your head isn't enough. The clarity you gain from documenting your plan, your values, your proposition and purpose is invaluable. As the company grows, you'll be further and further away from each team member, the message getting lost in translation as it passes from team member to team member like the baton in a relay race. Your memory will become foggy; the message won't be clear. People can't read your mind – you need to write down your brand strategy.

If you're planning to grow something bigger than you, put the time in now. Don't build your dream without its foundations. Let us show you how to create a brand strategy that can stand the test of time. You can decorate the walls later. You'll thank us later, too.

Competitor Analysis and Finding the White Space

Put simply, a brand strategy is how you differentiate yourself in the market to appeal to your specific customer. Strategy starts with identifying the 'white space', which is your point of difference to whoever is already in the market or a section of the market you can own. This is the most important part of your brand strategy. It's also often where we find we disagree the most with clients. Having been in brand and business building for a combined forty years, we have seen it all. This means that we can say with confidence that often your business is not as distinct as you think it is. That's why where product stops, the brand needs to begin, adding layers to the overall strategy to set you apart.

People often claim the white space doesn't exist anymore as the market is saturated, but we believe this is incorrect. If you're launching a brand into a crowded market, you need to find your differentiator, and your ownable white space. Without these, there is no point in launching at all.

As W. Chan Kim and Renée Mauborgne write in *Blue Ocean Strategy*, 'The idea that there are no more opportunities in saturated markets is a myth. Innovation and differentiation can always create new white space, even in the most crowded industries.'[1]

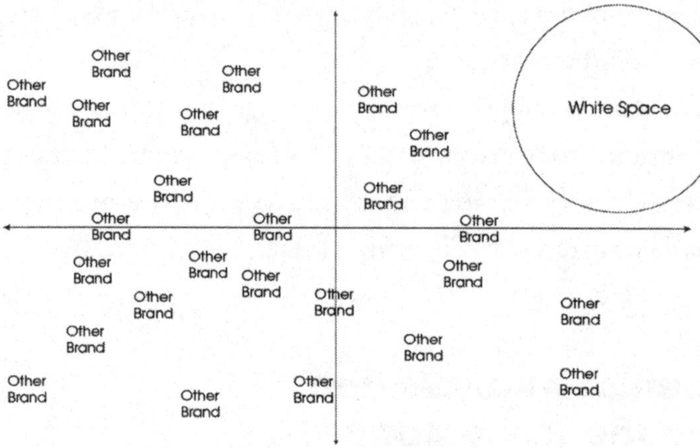

There are several steps involved in crafting a great brand strategy. Don't skip any.

Step 1: Find and Analyse Your Competitors

First, you have to find your competitors, but how do you do that? Here are some places to look:

- Retailers: Who are the potential stockists for your brand? From national chains to specialty stores, write them all down and then search their online stores and shelves by category. Take note of every brand that has a similar product offering to yours.
- Google and Amazon: Yep, just type in words that describe your brand and see what comes up.
- Social media: Instagram, Pinterest, TikTok, and YouTube are search engines in their own right. Use hashtags to search for content connected to brands in your space.
- Online reports: There are plenty of free resources online if you look hard enough. LinkedIn can be a great place to find them. A lot of companies use free resources as a lead generation opportunity – often, by giving them your email you get the report. You can unsubscribe later.
- Austrade: The Australian government has official departments designed to help Australian businesses from a local level all the way through to state and federal governments. Austrade is one of them. If you're not Australian, ask your local council for recommendations of government resources that can help you.
- Annual reports: Listed companies are required to make their annual reports public. All you have to do is google them and you'll instantly be learning from the best. Make yourself a cup of tea – they are usually long and sometimes boring, but there's always a nugget or two of wisdom in them.

When collecting information on your competitors, you want to understand a few key things:

- Price positioning: Where do they sit on a scale from cheap to affordable to expensive?
- Product benefits: Are they led by a particular hero ingredient, technology or benefit? Do they have multiple categories within their product range that offer customers different benefits?
- Brand positioning: Do they have a clear tagline or personality? How would you describe the brand's visual appearance and messaging in a few simple words?
- Market positioning: Are they appealing to mass consumer groups or are they targeting a particular demographic?

As you do your research, visit the websites and social pages of your competitors and read the messaging they provide to their customers to better understand how they want customers to perceive them. Then, spend a lot of time reading customer reviews and comments to understand how customers actually feel about the brand and the product.

While we didn't have direct competitors specifically for the coffee scrub (our hero product), we looked at the larger beauty industry and body care market as our competitors.

From a brand perspective, these markets were dominated by huge conglomerates and mass players. We scoured the body care aisles both in bricks and mortar stores and online, and we identified two categories among our competitors. One: clinical, pharmacy-focused brands with sans serif fonts, stark white packaging, blue and green accents and scary-looking scientific terms. Two: the natural category with cursive writing, eco-friendly packaging and often some kind of leaf icon (the epitome of greenwashing).

Our goal was always to take market share from the big conglomerates, not the smaller natural players. We weren't there to play small. We saw an opportunity for frank body to be a brand that was the antithesis of everything in the beauty and body care market. This was a radical new thing.

Our competitors were using superfluous, supercharged language. Their product names and descriptions read like science experiments, and often made big claims they couldn't back up. Trust us and every other millennial woman; we tried them all. Because of our experience as disappointed customers combined with our insight as strategists and copywriters, we decided our brand would use language that was transparent, upfront and frank, giving customers something truly unique from the category.

Our competitors spoke from a third-person perspective, often in cold, corporate and distant language. We decided to speak from a first-person perspective, being warm and engaging like a friend.

Their brand colours were blue and white. We were pink and coffee brown.

They were a feminine cliché. We were bold and cheeky.

They were playing in bricks and mortar retail and advertising through traditional channels like magazines and TV ads. We decided to start organically in a space they weren't even part of, going directly to our potential customers on social media.

The key to a good competitor analysis is to be unbiased. The benefits our competitors had over us were plentiful – they had built decades of brand awareness and had hefty marketing budgets, research teams and large retail distribution. The trust and credibility that came with a logo people immediately recognised was something we had to compete with from day one. To combat this, we focused on the key levers of speed and agility.

If you want to complete a strong competitor analysis that leads to actual insights, make sure you avoid these common mistakes:

Don't let your bias influence your analysis

It's easy to pick the flaws in your competitors or let your personal bias influence your insights. Look at your competitors objectively. What are they doing well? Why are customers coming to them? What can you learn?

Don't just look at direct competitors

It would have been easy for us to only focus on other body scrub brands, but that would have been doing ourselves a disservice. Instead, we looked at the wider beauty industry including the makeup and hair categories. We liked the energy and sexiness they brought to their branding and we thought, *Why not apply that same energy to skin care?*

Think about your direct and indirect competitors, complementary categories or contemporaries. Don't copy, but find insight and inspiration.

Don't forget to apply your strategic thinking

It's one thing to collate data – it's another to analyse it. Once you've looked at all the strengths and weaknesses of your competitors, you need to pull out the key learnings and opportunities for your brand. This could be an essential human truth you stumble across or a clear pattern you see emerging. Listen to your gut – that thing that told you to explore this idea in the first place – and back up your intuition with data.

Fill in the blanks ...					
	A new, healthy ice-cream brand	Brand A	Brand B	Brand C	Brand D
Price	Premium $2.80 per 100ml				
Benefits	Sugar free				
Market positioning	Premium, healthy but not sacrificing taste				
Audience	Millennials				
Colour palette	Six pastels				
Distribution	Grocery and premium food shops				
Strengths	Eye-catching design, good key selling point				
Weaknesses	Weak social media and marketing, low numbers of good reviews				
Personality	Bold, fun, friendly				

Plotting your competitors on a grid can be a handy exercise. You might also like to create multiple versions of the grid with different axes. Eventually you'll find your white space.

What do they bring to the table?

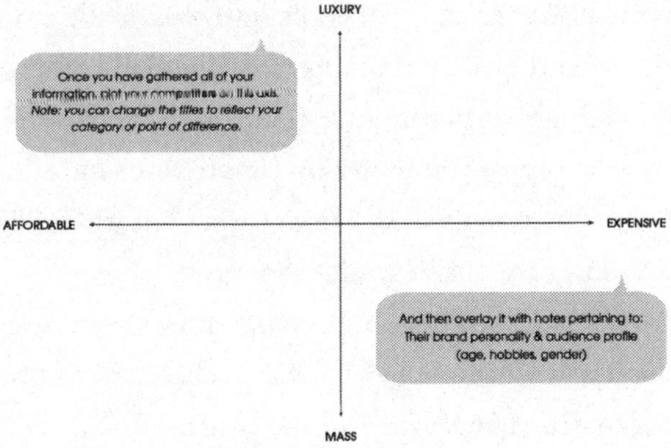

Step 2: Understand Your Audience

Your brand image exists within your customer's mind, and that means it's tangled up with their own perception of themselves. They reach for one brand over another because of what it says about them as a person.

For us, a strong brand is all about connection. Because, ultimately, people aren't just buying things, they buy into the story behind the words. By attempting to understand your customer – their values, feelings and ideals – you can better understand how to connect with them and make them feel something.

Audience analysis isn't just about looking broadly at your customers' demographics – sex, age and earning potential, for example. More importantly, audience analysis helps you understand your customers' psychographics – their wants, needs and desires. What makes them tick. At the end of the day, we're all humans trying to connect with something.

For frank body, we niched down. We're still big believers that for startups this is a strong strategy.

Our target customer was us: women in their early twenties interested in health and wellness. No one younger, no one older, although naturally they got caught in the content net, too. People started to make more conscious decisions about what they were drinking (less Red Bulls, more green juice); what they were eating (less two-minute noodles, more activated almonds); and what they were putting on their skin (less toxic chemicals, more clean ingredients). Our customer wasn't a high earner but was willing to invest in her health and beauty. Like we said, she was us.

To start, we documented our core demographic as a persona. We listed the brands she liked, what she did on the weekend, her values, her pain points, her purchasing behaviour and the platforms we would reach her on. We knew her inside out, and she was who we targeted religiously in the early years.

As we grew over the years, we added new demographic groups to target based on our research. We also evolved our current target demographic until we had three clear groups with distinct product strategies for each one.

We tested our assumptions about our audience through data analysis. As Chief Marketing Officer (CMO), Jess spent a *lot* of time in spreadsheets, the back end of Shopify and Google Analytics to ensure she knew who our customers were and could hypothesise who they could be. When we weren't behind our computers, we were conducting surveys via email, social and on the street. We were hosting customer meet-ups in our office. We were in retail stores learning from the floor staff. We were always asking questions. This allowed us to continually refine our view of who our customer was and evolve as she did.

Even though it was a good starting point, a key learning for us through frank body was not to assume your customer is the same as you. And not to assume your customer won't change over time. Our customer started out just like us, but as we changed so did she – and not always in the same ways. We had to learn how to cater for her, not only ourselves.

Many brands make this mistake. Remember that your brand will evolve and your customer will evolve. As you grow, you must keep being curious and open to adaptation.

There are many ways to document your audience. A good place to start is by identifying their pain point. That is, what problem do they have that you can solve? Next, go into their purchasing behaviours. Lastly, you must explore their values – the honest, revealing set of values they act on, not the ones they say they have.

As you grow, you can segment your audience into different categories, too. Some to think about are:

- first-time buyers versus repeat customers
- sale-conscious versus premium seekers
- active social followers versus referred buyers

Each audience group may have different wants and needs. As your data becomes more sophisticated, you can tailor their purchasing journey based on what you know about similar customers. For example, repeat customers could be rewarded for their loyalty with early access to new products, whereas first-time buyers might need an incentive like free shipping to convince them to make their first purchase.

Audience Persona Template

Persona Name: *Give them a name to humanise them (e.g. Fitness Fanatic, Beauty Junkie)*

Demographics

- Age:
- Gender:
- Location:
- Occupation:

Psychographics

- Lifestyle: *What kind of life do they live? Busy? Health-focused? Or more interested in margaritas than green smoothies?*
- Values: *What do they care about most? e.g. sustainability, saving money, looking snatched?*
- Interests/hobbies: *What do they do when they aren't working or studying? Hot mat Pilates, slam poetry, bed rotting?*

Pain Points and Challenges

- Lifestyle: *Where are they frustrated or stretched? What feels hard or makes them unable to lead the lifestyle they want?*
- Product/category specific: *Where are the current offerings falling short for them? What have they tried that hasn't worked? What can't they find?*
- Emotional: *What negative emotions does this audience have tied to this product/category? If they were complaining to a friend, what would they say?*

Goals and Motivations

- *What are they hoping to achieve when it comes to this product/ category?*
- *Why are they trying to achieve this? Need, joy, desire? Personal pride, societal expectations?*
- *How do they want to feel after solving the problem or challenge?*

Shopping and Decision-making Behaviour

- *Where do they research or shop? (e.g. Instagram, TikTok, Google, IRL)*
- *How do they decide what to buy? (e.g. reviews, endorsements, brand)*
- Price sensitivity: *(Low/medium/high)*

Media and Content Consumption

- Favorite social platforms:
- Preferred content formats: *(Short video, blog posts, podcasts, reviews, memes)*
- Influencers they follow:

Relationship to Your Brand

- How your product/brand fits into their life:
- What they're hoping to get from your brand:

Step 3: Define Your Mission and Find Your Purpose

Brand missions: The what, how and why

Most entrepreneurs we know are either a little crazy or naive. We were both. We had no preconceived ideas of how a beauty brand should be built, but we had the tenacity to think we could do it better than the multimillion-dollar beauty conglomerates. It turns out we were right. We had a clear mission.

Your brand mission is important because it helps everyone in your team (and everyone who could join it) work towards a common goal. Typically, your brand mission will be made up of three key elements:

- What: The specific products or services you provide.
- How: The way you deliver these products or services.
- Why: The underlying reason or motivation behind what you do.

As you grow and people make suggestions about new products and services you could create, it becomes hard to justify why you should or shouldn't follow their advice. Should your trucking company make wheels? Should your baby product brand make maternity clothes? Should your skincare brand make hair care? (We learned that one the hard way.) With a mission in place, you will have a safeguard in the decision-making process. Overlooking this can cost businesses a lot down the track.

Mistakes we made so you don't have to

Mistakes are the motivators behind writing this book: we want to impart our learnings so that you can avoid costly, stressful missteps. Why do we think this book matters? Because this isn't just theory. It's practice. It's knowledge acquired by creating a brand with your own money, your own skin in the game and your own house on the line. There are many marketing books out there already, many of which have some good ideas, but are often written by academics who have not grown a consumer brand with their own blood, sweat and tears from the ground up. This is why we believe it's important for founders to share their stories, because a rising tide can lift all boats.

The steps to defining your brand mission don't need to be complicated, but they do need to be considered carefully:

1. Define your core offering clearly (*what*).
2. Identify your unique approach or method (*how*).
3. Articulate the deeper purpose that drives your business (*why*).
4. Ensure it aligns with your brand values and target audience.
5. Keep it clear, concise and actionable.

Brand purpose: A reason for existing beyond profit

A brand purpose goes beyond simply selling products or services. It's the fundamental reason for a brand's existence beyond financial profit, encompassing the impact you aim to have or the value you aim to create in the world. Brands that stand for something deeper earn a place in consumers' lives far quicker than those that are focused on beating their competitors and being 'the best'.

Put simply, the question you need to ask yourself is: why should your brand exist?

When we asked ourselves this question for frank body, the answer was clear. We wanted to create a brand for our generation. We were the generation that had grown up being told they could be anything and now felt an expectation to be *everything*. A generation that grew up with Victoria's Secret and models with perfect skin squeezing imaginary pimples and shaving already hairless legs. We were fed a radical diet of fat-free perfectionism that left many young women feeling less-than. We wanted to create a brand that was real, honest and, well … frank. A brand that made people feel great not just through great products, but through content that was the antithesis of everything we had been raised on.

Our core brand purpose became: 'To make babes feel great.'

The concept of making the customer feel great extended into everything we did. We always aimed to make her smile, feel empowered or feel strong – emotionally and physically. We built a community around frank body that was inclusive, progressive and authentic. We assumed our customers were smart and wanted more than just skincare tips. Instead of the same tired content, we gave them content around all the issues that were important in their life: money, sex, relationships, career progression, mental health. No topic was off limits – in fact, the more taboo the better.

When discovering your purpose, there are a few things to keep in mind:

- Meaningful impact: Aim to articulate the broader societal or human impact that your brand aspires to make.
- Emotional connection: It's time to get deep. Your purpose should resonate with emotions and aim to connect with your audience. It's not just about what your brand does but why it does it.

- Alignment with values: Your purpose should align with the brand values you've already created.
- Authenticity and commitment: An authentic brand purpose isn't merely a marketing ploy; it's ingrained in the brand's culture and operations. It must be backed by tangible actions.

Remember, your brand purpose is your north star, so it should be tweaked, altered and toyed with as little as possible.

In *The Founder Playbook* podcast with Emma Grede on 13 May 2025, Mike Rubin (founder of Fanatics) mentioned that he didn't originally place importance on identifying the brand's mission, but in hindsight he wished he had.[2] It wasn't until after a (rather large) issue with a new product release that Rubin was forced to review how and why they made products. Finally, Fanatics developed the company mission: 'To relentlessly improve the fans' experience.' On the podcast, Rubin reflected that he wished he had realised the importance of defining the mission sooner – because he believes he could have built a bigger and better company.

Step 4: Define Your Brand Pillars

The final elements that we include in a brand strategy are the brand pillars. These are sometimes known as 'brand values' – however, we have found that the word 'values' often results in a cutting room floor of one hundred clichéd words rather than ideas that are unique and robust. The brand pillars become the guiding principles that will direct your brand forwards. Think of them as guardrails for what is important on a structural level. If you think of your brand as a house, then the brand pillars are the frame that ensures the brand is strong and unlikely to blow over.

Brand pillars are not customer-facing, but they are reflected in everything your brand does. Your team should know your brand pillars and ensure that they are reflected in everything your brand says, does or is associated with.

The brand pillars we developed for frank body were:

HONESTY

'I take a frank approach to everything from communications to formulations. I aim to have honest and open conversations with my frankfurts (what we called our customers and fans, which yes – did confuse some of our German customers) at all times.'

INTEGRITY

'I use seriously great ingredients to make seriously good products that do what they say, with no empty promises.'

FUN

'I believe skin care should be enjoyable. Even though our products deliver serious benefits, we don't take ourselves too seriously.'

INCLUSIVITY

'I believe everybody is a babe, and everyone should have access to skin care that works for them. We break beauty standards down, and we have since day one.'

These values have fundamentally stayed the same since we launched in 2013. Your values should be:

- Short: There's no point in having ten brand values that no one remembers. Keep them concise and memorable.
- Timeless: Your values should be ones you are willing to fight for

time and time again. They are bigger than one person and should stand the test of time.

- Meaningful: You can't randomly choose nouns from a list. Think about values you can put into action.

What's at the core of it all?

Knowing what you and your audience values is always a good place to start. Start with a big list of values and strength test each one until you have four remaining. Only four. No more.

If you can remember these values when asked off the cuff, that's a good indication they are right.

If you can't, perhaps you need to question their authenticity.

Remember that brand pillars don't need to be written as single words. You can use sentences or phrases. As long as they resonate and are memorable.

Now you have your white space, your audience, your pillars and your purpose.

You might like to add a brand proposition and or a brand archetype to this.

A brand proposition is a clear statement that communicates your brand's unique value and what sets it apart from competitors. It shows why customers should choose your brand over others.

A brand archetype is a universal character or personality type that your brand embodies. The idea is based on Carl Jung's twelve primary archetypes (like the Hero, the Caregiver or the Rebel) and helps create a consistent, relatable brand personality that resonates with your target audience.

Both these elements can strengthen your brand strategy by providing additional clarity and direction for your brand's positioning and personality. Remember, though, you don't need to have a perfect pyramid or a brand triangle to have a successful brand – you need to know who you are and why you exist, and ensure anyone who works with you understands it too.

Let's review:

- The competitors: Who your customers are choosing between.
- The mission: What you do, how you do it, and who it serves.
- The purpose: The reason you exist beyond profit.
- The proposition: Your unique selling point.
- The audience: The specific subset of people who will be the target of your marketing.

THE LESSON:

The best ideas are rooted in strategy.

Chapter 6

THE BUILDING BLOCKS OF A BRAND: NAME, TONE OF VOICE AND VISUAL IDENTITY

In the year Jess was born, her name topped the list of most popular girls' names. Approximately one in thirty girls during the eighties and nineties were named Jessica. Jess doesn't dislike her name, although now most people call her J. Jess did dislike having to use the first letter of her surname to identify herself because there were so many Jessicas at her school. She could never just be Jess, she was always Jess H. It drove her mad that it wasn't immediately obvious who was being spoken to or about when she heard the name 'Jess' or 'Jessica'. To her, this is the perfect anecdote to explain the importance of crafting a unique name and tone of voice for your brand. You want your brand to be a Phoenix, Opal or

Cosmo in a sea of Jessicas. And yes, naming our children was the most high-pressure branding exercise of our lives.

What's in a Name?

At Willow & Blake, our process for naming brands and developing their tone of voice is to always start with a strategic insight. If you don't know why you're doing it then that funny quip you've made won't stand the test of time.

The most asked question about frank body is: 'Why did you call it that?'

By now you understand what the beauty landscape looked like at the time of frank body's inception. We identified what our white space was, we knew our reason for existing and our pillars, and next we needed to work out exactly how to execute a brand that would fulfil all of our objectives; one that was different in every way, shape and form to the incumbents of the category. And we needed to do all this without alienating our potential customers. We spent many days in the Willow & Blake office brainstorming – upside down on our second-hand chesterfield couches spitballing ideas; sprawled across the floor with our chunky 2010-era silver MacBooks; sometimes sitting in coffee shops eating our beloved overpriced avocado toast. Somehow, no matter what idea we threw out there, nothing felt quite as sticky as our very first instinct: exploring the concept of frankness. Once we decided on this as a central feature of the brand, each sentence we uttered built on the former with ease. The conversation went something like this:

- We know that customers like us want honesty and transparency from brands – they are sick of false claims. Let's be frank about what our product does.

- Customers also want to hear about things other than products. Could this brand be frank about everything from relationships to career, body image, and the very industry we are part of?
- We want to use Instagram to launch the brand. Could the concept of being 'frank' become a character? Could the brand talk in first person to integrate into the platform naturally?

And so the character of frank was born and so too was their cheeky, innuendo-riddled tone of voice. We had insights about the beauty industry and knew the feeling our customers had – they were disenfranchised with it. We coupled this with the distribution strategy for our content. By bringing those things together, we reached this moment – without this strategic thinking and the foundation upon which the brand was built, it just wouldn't have made sense. This is why the copycats that came soon after our launch didn't last. A brand called 'Bob Scrub' simply didn't cut the mustard.

The concept of frankness was deeply embedded in our brand's DNA. Not only did it take pride of place, front and centre as the brand name, but it was also within everything we created for the brand. frank body was an ecosystem that orbited around the very word at the centre of it all: frank.

When it comes to naming a brand, there are many methods available, and we explore them all when creating brands for our clients at Willow & Blake.

- Descriptive names: These directly describe what the product or service does (e.g. Australia Post, Commonwealth Bank). It is helpful for some categories, but the same understanding of a service can be achieved through good supporting copy and keywords for most brands in the digital age.
- Founder names: This is when we use the name of the company's founder or founders (e.g. Disney, Ford). If there is a great story

and the founder is planning to stay with the brand for a long time, this can be a wonderful method. However, you are putting all of your metaphorical eggs in one basket, and it can make it difficult to separate the brand from the founder in the event of an exit.

- Acronyms: This method takes the initials of a longer name to create something shorter and more memorable (e.g. IBM, BMW). This concept is a bit meh, in our humble opinion. It often feels cold and corporate.
- Suggestive names: These are names that hint at the brand's benefits or attributes without directly stating them (e.g. Netflix, Pinterest). This is a great method for building something unique and category-defining, often with the goal of building the word into a verb rather than a noun over time, as in 'Netflix and chill'.
- Invented words or coined language: This method creates entirely new words that sound interesting and are guaranteed to be unique (e.g. Kodak, Xero). We are particularly fond of this naming approach, as it makes it easier to find unique domain names, social handles and trademarks. It makes it easier to find you on Google – ironically, another coined term. This misspelling of 'googol' (the number 1 followed by 100 zeros) was picked to signify that the search engine was intended to provide large quantities of information.
- Foreign words: This is when we use words from other languages that relate to the brand's essence (e.g. Nike, Samsung). When it's executed well, this is brilliant – however, it runs the risk of being cliché or difficult to spell, which is terrible for website traffic. In the worst case, this approach could land you with something that's culturally insensitive.
- Metaphorical names: This involves using symbols or metaphors that represent the brand's values (e.g. Amazon, Apple). This is a fantastic method for developing a brand with values deeply embedded in every layer – a value cake, if you will.

- Geographic names: These names use locations associated with the brand (e.g. AriZona Tea, American Express). We find this pretty boring and hard to build upon, much like descriptive names. However, it can be suitable and executed well, as is the case with Patagonia.
- Combination names: Merging two words or concepts to create something new (e.g. Facebook, Instagram). This is another favourite at Willow & Blake for the same reasons as invented words.
- Experiential names: These are names that evoke a feeling or experience (e.g. Boost Juice, Rip Curl). This is a strong method that allows you to build on an emotion and really connect with customers. It usually inspires lots of content themes and marketing ideas, too.

Each naming strategy has its own advantages and considerations. The key is selecting a method that aligns with your brand's strategy, values, distribution and target audience while ensuring the name is:

- memorable
- easy to pronounce and spell
- available for trademark, domain names and social handles
- culturally appropriate across markets
- suitable for digital platforms.

Then there is the cutting room floor – a copywriter's graveyard of great but not-quite-right names. Every copywriter has a cutting room floor full of ideas (usually in their notes app) that they hope one day will perfectly fit the brief they are presented with.

For every brand builder, there are names that stick with them forever – these are the ones that make them proud every time they are referenced or seen in the wild. Here are some of our highlights:

Bouf

For this haircare brand name, we turned two dials. First, the implication of strength, growth and hair health. Then, the use of humour, personality and a dash of chaos. We landed on 'Bouf'. An onomatopoeic name that sounds exactly like what it's offering: big hair. Fun to say, short and with potential for big visual impact.

Cattywampus

A project that is still one of our favourites. This brand produces beautifully crafted tiny tents for kids' bedrooms, designed to inspire imaginative play. We dove into this concept headfirst – this was long before we had children of our own. 'Cattywampus' means something that is in disarray or that is askew – like the inside of a child's mind. To adults, it won't make sense. It may even be considered wrong. But this is imagination's playground, where there are no rules and doing things differently is encouraged.

NOYA

A nut butter brand from Brunswick that's popular all over the world. Inspired by Soho, which stands for 'South of Houston Street', we created NOYA, which stands for 'North of the Yarra' – a reference to the company's warehouse location in Brunswick.

Future Future

This cult restaurant in Richmond, Melbourne had a strong sense of self from day one. A purpose defined by its founders and their incredible creative instincts led us down an exploratory path of all things Japanese – both the deep-seated traditions and their obsessiveness with the future.

Developing a Brand's Tone of Voice

Tone of voice, which is how a brand sounds, is an important bridge between your brand strategy and the name. This is where many brands go wrong – by copying what is working well for someone else, playing it too safe or (on the opposite end of the spectrum) being so esoteric that no one gets it. 'Tone of voice' is called that for a reason: it sets the tone for everything your brand does moving forward, from your packaging to your customer service emails to your website description to the pitch you put together for investors or retailers. These words are the glue holding your business together.

frank body and nudity are a package deal. Our customer was naked when they used the product, so the language and tone of voice followed suit (specifically, the birthday suit). It was cheeky, bordering on taboo, but also relatable, like a friend you've known for years with whom no topic is off limits. Context is important when we talk about sexual innuendo and cheek. Due to the intimate nature of using our product, these things made sense for our brand. Selling someone a Chiko Roll with a half-naked woman on a motorbike? Not so much. The frank body voice broke through the dullness of the body category like a wrecking ball, shattering all previously held notions of what it meant to be a beauty or personal care brand. It was an invitation to women everywhere to embrace those things they'd previously been shamed for. Instead of reinforcing shame, we put that inner monologue on public display and celebrated it. And our customers did the best thing we could have ever hoped for: emulating the brand's voice in their social content. Naturally, the frank body voice evolved over time as the brand matured, but it has never strayed too far from its origins.

Here are six key steps for developing a distinctive brand tone of voice:

1. Define your brand personality: Identify 3–5 key personality characteristics that reflect your brand's values and mission. The most important rule: don't be generic. 'Trustworthy' is a basic expectation of being in business, not a value that sets you apart.
2. Use toggles or spectrums: If you run into issues deciding on your brand's personality traits (especially if there are multiple co-founders), create sliding scales between opposing traits (like casual versus formal, or playful versus serious) to help you work out where you want your brand to sit.
3. Fact over feeling: Despite intuition being an important part of brand building, 'I feel' and 'I think' are not valid sentence-starters in the world of brand building, as they set a conversation up for failure. After all, how can someone really rebut your feelings? Replace these common negotiation tactics with 'the insight shows' and 'the strategy tells us', and you'll get to a logical outcome much quicker.
4. Establish content pillars: What will your brand stand for beyond product? What will you talk about with customers to drive engagement? Develop a series of 2–5 non-product content pillars to flesh out your content strategy across your site, socials and email. These are different to your brand pillars. Think of brand values as the foundational principles that guide how the company makes decisions, while content pillars are the actual topics and themes you discuss with your audience to demonstrate those values.
5. Map out the customer journey: You need to adapt the tone for different communication channels, but it doesn't mean you dilute the brand or dull things down and do it the way everyone else does. Moments to surprise and delight your customer are key, so leave no stone unturned. We've seen some beautiful work on the underside of a shipping box or in a confirmation email.
6. Develop word banks: Create lists of approved and prohibited words that align with the brand voice. This can often help the copywriter

and team around them to maintain consistency and cement 'who' the brand is. An example for us is our bone-deep hatred of exclamation marks. They are a lazy way of emphasising something. An upside-down exclamation mark, however, is brilliant¡¡¡¡

The keys to successful tone of voice development are consistency and authenticity, but even more important is *originality*. Your brand voice should feel thought-provoking, natural and reflective of your brand's true personality rather than mimicking competitor voices or following trending styles. Nailing this will help you create the long-lasting emotional entanglement you need to build a cult brand.

Bri Nixon – Creative Director, Willow & Blake
On developing DISSH's tone of voice

I rock up to the office in my DISSH black pants and signature red jumper, hoping genius isn't like lightning – I need it to strike again.

The DISSH team came to us for a sprint – a refined brand strategy and tone of voice before a big trip to New York. High stakes. Short runway.

I had to crack it and crack it fast.

I already knew how the brand had transformed over the years. From Gold Coast clubwear to chic, minimalist staples. From our first call, I got the rest of their story. Values-driven with the claims to prove it: parental-leave initiatives, environmental responsibility, pride scholarship, charity partners, circularity. It goes on.

The product was already pulling its weight, the team doing everything right. Now the words needed to do the same.

The opportunity lifted its head and stuck out its tongue. I needed to inject more personality into the copywriting.

But what does 'more personality' mean, anyway?

Spike the words with fierce femininity (do not read as 'girly').

Channel effortless cool (like its home state, the sunshine one).

And always be considered (not superior, but sincere).

Inspiration came from Reformation's killer tagline, 'Being naked is the #1 most sustainable option. Reformation is #2'. Plus frank body's promise, 'The most fun you can have in the bathroom'. And Glossier's mantra, 'Skin first. Makeup second'.

I thought DISSH could afford to hold its head a little higher after everything they'd achieved. So I added a sprinkle of sass.

'Your clothes say a lot about you. We make sure it's all good.'

I loved this line. Still do. But we ultimately wanted it shorter. More elevated. Editorial. A tagline that emphatically nods to the conscious thought that goes on behind the scenes at DISSH. Something with rhythm and flow. We landed on the tagline: 'Shop intentionally. Style effortlessly.'

Then we rolled out the brand voice.

Boring: 'Women's clothing for every event on your social calendar.'

Way better: 'Considered clothing you don't have to consider.'

Yawn-fest: 'New season has landed. Be quick and shop now.'

On point: 'Oh no, our new season has landed. And it's full of must-haves.'

Kind of funny: 'If it's not DISSH, it's probs shit.'

Hits the right note: 'So sorry to all your other clothes.'

I gave the team a toolkit to match. From HQ to shop floor, we rolled out the new tone and trained them on the language tools and rules. Here's the skinny:

- Don't be sexual or crass.
- Don't overuse pop culture; it's low-hanging fruit.

- Don't be passive.
- Don't use exclamation marks.
- Use hyperbole. Example: 'Wear in infinite combinations.'
- Employ metaphors. Example: 'Feeling blue? Cheer up, our best-selling winter coat is now in navy.'
- Be witty. Example: 'You may not have it all together. But your outfit does.'

And then it was in the capable hands of the DISSH team to keep alive. A breathing, talking brand voice that will no doubt grow up one day. But they'll always have the guidelines.

I could show you them, but then I'd have to kill you.

Scroll their captions. Scoop their emails. Read the voice in action. See what happens when your words dress as well as you do.

Building a Brand's Visual Identity

'Being a graphic designer is like being a chef where everyone watches cooking shows and thinks they're Gordon Ramsay. They'll look at your work and say "make the logo bigger" just like they'd tell a chef to "add more salt" without tasting the dish.'

– Paul Rand[3]

The very fun and often fiddly aspect of creating your brand's visual identity comes next, often at the cost of a graphic designer's soul or sanity. Or both.

If done correctly, the visual identity should be a natural extension of the strategy, drawing on the same insights as the name and tone of voice to build a holistic brand where the colours, typography, patterns and design tools further embed the brand values and personality. Random colours and fonts on a page do not make a visual identity. This is often one of the most difficult parts of a brand to execute without a professional. We generally recommend engaging a designer to create your visual identity after all the strategy and tone of voice work is done. They can always create templates for you to work with later to assist with costs.

A creative director or graphic designer will generally take the following steps to build a brand's visual identity:

1. Define core visual elements: This involves establishing a primary logo, secondary marks, colour palette, typography and imagery style that align with the brand strategy and personality.
2. Refine the colourway: This is when a designer decides on the primary, secondary and accent colours that work across digital and print applications, ensuring accessibility and uniqueness in your category. To do this well, we suggest mapping out as much of the distribution and product strategy as possible. If you plan to introduce new product lines or categories down the track, colours can greatly impact how this rolls out.
3. Lock in the font: This is formally known as 'typography', or colloquially as 'font'. This is when we select and define typography rules for headline, body and accent fonts that enhance readability and brand recognition.
4. Assess the application: Ensuring that the visual elements work across all sizes and platforms – from favicon to billboard – is key to a strong visual identity, so this is when a designer will strength test the concept.
5. Develop style guidelines: This is when a designer creates comprehensive brand guidelines that detail usage rules, dos and don'ts and application examples. This can also extend to

photography style, illustration approach and iconography systems to maintain consistency.

The key to successful visual identity development is creating a system that is:

- distinctive and ownable
- flexible across applications
- future-proof and adaptable
- easy to implement consistently
- aligned with your brand strategy, name and tone of voice.

Remember that the visual identity should evolve with your brand while maintaining its core essence. Regular audits and updates ensure the system remains relevant and effective. Rebrands should be left to the professionals, and should only happen when a very clear business case is put forward that highlights the needs and benefits of a rebrand; sometimes they are crucial, but sometimes they are a lazy marketer's way of stamping their mark on the business.

When the Visual Identity Goes Wrong

The agency that developed the original frank body visual identity brand gave us the bare bones of brand – which was all we could afford at the time. It looked cute and appealed to our target audience, but it lacked future-proofing – because when we went to build out new SKUs eighteen months later there was no flexibility in the colour palette, lock ups and patterns to extend beyond what already existed in the portfolio. Willow & Blake didn't do design at that point in time, but it was the catalyst for us to take on the role of creative director and redesign the brand's visual identity, including logo, pattern, colour palette, packaging and typography with our internal designer. We are forever thankful to the team of designers we had in house, who were patient, understanding, solutions-oriented and risk-taking as we worked hand in hand to redo the visual identity of the brand in a way that allowed us to carefully and thoughtfully expand our product range. They helped make frank body what it is today.

THE LESSON:

If you don't believe it, neither will anyone else. Be original, be genuine, be consistent.

Chapter 7

CREATING A COMMUNITY OF RAVING FANS

The night we launched, our site crashed due to too much traffic and we sold out of product.

Anyone who has launched a business through Shopify will know there is nothing more satisfying than the buzz of seeing your first order come through. We launched frank body on a normal Thursday night without any fanfare. There was no big launch party or special event. We simply put our very basic Shopify site live and posted an announcement on our Instagram page. Then we all got on with our nights.

Before launch, we'd built up our Instagram audience to over 10,000 followers – all organic growth from 24-hour-a-day content and hashtags. For a week before launch, we'd been teasing the product to the audience we had built instead of launching our product into the ether. This meant that when it was available to purchase, our first few orders came through quickly. They were from a mix of friends and strangers. We had no expectations, so this initial burst was a pleasant surprise and gave us a sense that we were on the right track. It seemed crazy to us that someone we'd never met had just purchased our product – a product we had made by hand, through a website we had built – after seeing the marketing we had created. Keep in mind that none of the founders had any prior experience in the beauty industry. These first few orders were enough to confirm that at least a few people were intrigued by what we were doing. Little did we know what was to come. An hour later, another order came through, then another and another. The dings kept coming and didn't stop. We'd been hopeful for some early success, but this was beyond expectations. Before long, a large key opinion leader ('influencers' weren't a thing yet) had posted about the product and directed their army of product-hungry twenty-somethings to our page. They were eager, going straight to our site and ordering multiple scrubs.

Eventually the dings stopped and a DM popped up on our Instagram.

Your website is down.

We had so much traffic that our site crashed. It was perhaps a fortunate accident, as we'd already oversold the 150 pre-made units. We looked at each other, grinning with the realisation that this humble little coffee scrub might actually be *something*.

Then the fear hit with the realisation that we needed to figure out how we were going to pack and send these orders – while also getting back in the kitchen to make more scrub.

The months that would follow were a blur of late nights and coffee grinds. We worked our normal day jobs from 9am to 5pm, then after work we made the product by hand in our apartment, stickered and labelled it, packed the scrubs into envelopes, and added the addresses. We then loaded the boxes into a supermarket trolley and wheeled them down to the post office.

Everything was covered in coffee – our clothes, hair, bedsheets, the floor. It was not glamourous. It was exhausting physically, mentally and emotionally, but the adrenaline was addictive. Or perhaps it was the coffee. Who knows.

Our co-founders Alex and Steve started to stay up later and later into the night (and early hours of the morning) making the scrub. At first, they stopped at 12am, then 1am, and when the packing took them into the early mornings and they still couldn't meet demand, we started to recruit more help.

Four months in, we got too big for the apartment and set up a workshop in a very cold, very dark warehouse in South Yarra. We gathered friends and family to help us pack. We supplied wine, pizza, movies and an hourly rate. We purchased a cement mixer that we affectionately called 'Frank the Tank' to help us make the scrub in bulk.

Steve's dedicated, ever-supportive parents ran the day crew. Steve and Alex ran the night crew. We stepped away from packing and focused on growing the brand, creating and posting content every single hour and emailing thousands – yes, thousands – of influencers and bloggers.

It was a happy day when on 18 December – just before Christmas – we eventually outsourced manufacturing to a local manufacturer, who we still use today. In January 2014, we outsourced fulfilment.

Our growth trajectory was exceptional. We paid back our initial investment (less than $10,000) one week after we launched. We hit 500,000 Instagram followers and made over $10 million in revenue in our first calendar year. It's important to note that our monetary investment was low because our sweat investment was high – we did everything ourselves. If we didn't know how to do it, we figured it out. A quick review of our search history from early 2013 would reveal this to be true ('How to send products from Australia to the US'). Now, the expectations of brands to be more polished at launch is the norm. You can absolutely bootstrap things, but an element of credibility is expected after the direct-to-consumer (DTC) boom.

The early days and months of the business were a wild time. frank body took over our lives and became our major focus while we also continued to run Willow & Blake. We sacrificed a lot that first year – our mental health, physical health, relationships. But most importantly, we survived.

How to Build a Community

You've heard the saying, 'build it and they will come'.

We totally disagree. Absolutely not. Once you launch, then the real work starts. You can't launch a brand and expect people to come to you. You have work to earn your customers. Every day, every year. The work doesn't stop.

There were three key factors that contributed to frank body and Willow & Blake's early growth: community, content and influencers.

On Community

People often assume it was just influencers that built our brand and led to our rapid growth. While their glossy photos and large followings certainly helped, they were not our secret weapon.

The secret to our success was our army of 'frankfurts' and #thefrankeffect. With every order we sent, we asked our customers to share their experience – and they did. From our inbox to our Instagram page, we were flooded with selfies of our customers covered in the scrub, before-and-afters of their skin and flat lays or shelfies of their frank body products artfully arranged. We owe our success to these early adopters.

When starting a brand, you must always think of your community and your customers first. It doesn't matter what your industry or product is. The end consumer is the queen (or king). If you earn their trust, they will become your biggest supporters. And if you can create an army of supporters, their endorsements are even more valuable. If you see an influencer post about a product, you assume it's probably been sponsored or that the influencer has an ulterior motive for posting. On the other hand, if a girlfriend tells you about this new scrub she's found or posts about it online, you know it must be because she genuinely loves it.

These days, this is known as 'the customer economy'.

The customer economy on social media is a system where regular customers are incentivised to promote brands, with monetary rewards based on the reach of their content. For example, brands might offer payments like $100 for every 10,000 views generated by customer-created content. This approach turns everyday consumers into brand advocates, creating a more authentic and relatable form of marketing compared to traditional influencer partnerships.

We didn't pay our customers to post about our products. So how did we convince hundreds of thousands of babes to cover themselves in coffee scrub and post about it on their Instagram? Let's break it down.

Step 1: Stand for something

People need a brand they can believe in. They buy into the story, not just the product. We positioned ourselves as mavericks. frank body was here to disrupt the stale beauty industry and make skin care fun. People wanted to be a part of that.

Step 2: Make it cool

Normalise it. Make it look like everyone is doing it. When we launched, it wasn't common for people to share their bathroom rituals across social media let alone post photos of themselves covered in coffee scrub. We created the trend. It started with our own pictures. Of our legs, feet, arms. Different angles, different bathrooms. Rarely our faces. We created a bank of content that could have been anyone, so it looked like everyone. It became a joke that every bathroom we visited we would put a scrub in the shower and snap a pic. We showed people how to create the content we wanted.

Step 3: Ask for what you want

We involved our frankfurts in every stage of the brand. We didn't just talk at them; we listened to them. We asked them questions and made them a part of the brand – from focus groups to Facebook groups to asking everyone who ordered to share their experience. And we shared their responses. Our Instagram wasn't post after post of models and influencers. We posted our customers before it was normal. This triggered more people wanting to post in the hopes they would also be featured.

Community and customers are everything, so this is where everything must start.

On Content

'Content' is everything you create on behalf of the brand – think campaign imagery, copy, emails, blogs, flyers, advertisements and, of course, social media posts.

We've always invested in content. Our very first marketing spend was on a photographer and model for our launch campaign shoot. We used a friend of ours who had a talent for capturing movement and emotion. He found a model who embodied everything frank body stood for. She wasn't signed with an agency or your typical size 8 with perfect skin. She was gorgeous, bold and knew how to work the camera. We shot in a local park where the model and her boyfriend ran through the woods like nymphs in their undies, covered in scrub. We then went back to the photographer's apartment and shot in the shower. Let's just say it got steamy. These images embodied frank body perfectly: fun, diverse, cheeky and bold. And they still adorn the walls of our office today.

We used these images for our website, flyers, press and social media. They set the tone for the brand. To supplement our campaign images, we went hard on lo-fi and sourced content. Our content pillars were fluid, but we were strict on one rule: don't just talk about the product. To start, our split was 80/20: 80 per cent lifestyle and 20 per cent product and sales messaging. We posted about bathrooms, coffee, babes, fitness, wellness and memes.

We were constantly glued to our phones, creating and curating content. We posted every hour on the hour, every day, 365 days a year. We posted on Christmas Day and New Year's Eve. If we didn't post, sales dropped. When we posted, sales came in. It made posting addictive. We started setting an alarm so we would wake up and post at 3am to hit the US market.

We do not recommend this strategy today.

Beyond Instagram, we did what we did best – we wrote. We started a blog and wrote about all the things our audience was interested in, like wellness, relationships, sex, fashion and interviews with influencers. No topic was off limits.

We started to build an email list and repurposed our blog posts for EDMs. These are all basic tricks and tools of content marketing, but they can't be overlooked.

As we got bigger, we were able to invest more in our campaign shoots and content. We were fortunate to work with incredible photographers, videographers, stylists and models from all around the world. Some were famous; some up and coming. All were incredibly creative and passionate. We shot everything from full-scale television commercials to out-of-home (OOH) campaigns. We did everything from filling a bathtub with over a hundred packets of marshmallows to filling a whole bathroom with helium balloons. We were constantly thinking of new ways to make our content stand out. When this book was written, our focus on high-production shoots had come full circle, back to a focus on mid-fi and lo-fi content.

For Bree, it's not just the biggest shoots that stand out in her memory. One of her favourite creative shoots was a blind casting call. This was a smaller campaign where we ran a competition for a community member to feature in one of our campaign shoots. The catch was that you didn't submit any photos and no judges could see the contestants. Instead, every babe was judged on their answer to one important question: 'What's a message worth sharing?'

Thousands of entries poured in from every corner of the globe with babes everywhere sharing important messages about hope, equal rights, inclusion and diversity. The winner was a mum from Western Australia named Fallon Gregory-Giles, whose heartfelt message about diversity and inclusion stood out among thousands of entries. We flew her to Sydney to shoot with Yasmin Suteja. We had no idea what she looked like until she walked through the doors.

She was beautiful inside and out. It was one of the riskiest but most rewarding shoots we did.

Our key tips for creating content that connects

Know your platform

It used to drive us crazy that our beautiful high-production campaign imagery would never perform as well on social media as a lo-fi iPhone image or video. But instead of repeating the same mistake again and again, we recognised that different content serves different purposes, and as a brand you must invest accordingly. We still believe in investing in high and low content. Campaign imagery works for retailers, web and visual marketing channels like OOH; whereas for social and digital channels, mid-fi or lo-fi tends to perform best.

Depending on your budget and your skill set, you may need to tailor your channels to the type of content you can create yourself or the type of content you can afford to have created for you. If you love the camera, learn how to edit your own video content or find a great editor and go hard on TikToks and reels. If you prefer to be off camera, try Instagram or LinkedIn. Remember, though, these days it is beneficial for founders to be front-facing.

If we were starting out, we would choose a couple of key channels and do them really well. The demand for content is insatiable, and if you try to commit to every channel at once you won't be able to maintain the quality or quantity of content needed.

Test and learn

We posted a lot. Some posts did well while others did not. We constantly adjusted our content plan to prioritise what people wanted to see. Knowing what content will perform is about understanding your audience, reading the cultural cues of the moment and not being afraid to try things.

Often, we see brands jumping on trends too late or trying to replicate content that's worked well for other brands, then not seeing the same results. In the world of social media there's a constant balance between speed and quality. We like to say, 'Done is better than perfect'. If you overthink a post or sit on it for too long, the moment will pass. Often the best content ideas are developed on the fly.

Be consistent but don't be generic

Another important factor when it comes to growth through content is consistency. We were on brand until it hurt. We knew our tone of voice – it was bold, distinctive and we never broke character. From the copy you read on our website to the social captions on Instagram to the box your order arrived in: everything was on brand.

Our tone of voice is cheeky, frank and always in the first person. A simple example is a line about animal testing that appears on all our packaging.

Most brands say, 'We don't test on animals'. frank body says, 'Tested on babes, not bunnies'.

Another example is our lip balms.

In the 'how to use' section we could talk like a generic brand and say to apply liberally to your lips as needed throughout the day.

But at frank body we say, 'If you have lips, you know how'.

Because let's be frank – everyone knows how to use lip balm.

Consistency builds trust. Don't be afraid to repeat key lines over and over again. For frank body and a lot of our Willow & Blake clients, we won't use a single tagline. Instead, we'll create a bank of key phrases and ownable terms, and we'll use these brand cues again and again. This repetition is very intentional, and must be consistent across all your content – from your website to your packaging to your marketing materials.

You don't have to be funny and cheeky like frank body, but do find your own angle and don't be vanilla. We don't need more brands playing it safe or creating cookie-cutter content. Find your point of difference and run with it.

Create a plan

Once you start, it's never-ending. You must feed the engine. To ensure you don't run out of ideas, it can help to create a plan. This might look like a marketing plan or a content calendar. Don't only talk about your product. It's easy for new launches to dictate your marketing calendar, but ensure you allow for pure brand moments – those times that your brand values, not product and promotions – to come to the forefront and take the limelight throughout the year.

Work with great people

Putting together a great team for a creative project is a joy. There are so many talented people out there who want to create great work. Don't settle for average – find the people who understand your vision and can elevate it, and work with them. In the digital age, this also means looking globally. You don't have to have huge budgets to be creative; see what you can do yourself, invest in a camera, learn to use AI, and upskill in art direction. We have loved using up-and-coming photographers and models.

How Do You Create Groundswell?

'Key opinion leaders'. 'Influencers'. 'Content creators'. 'Brand ambassadors'. They've been called a lot of things. Put simply, these are people with the power to affect the opinions, behaviours or purchasing decisions of other people.

Think what you want of influencers, their power is undeniable. In 2025 (when writing this), influencers are getting roles in movies, creating Super Bowl ads and commanding fees akin to a yearly salary for a single TikTok.

A survey by marketing agency HigherVisibility in 2022 found one in four Gen Zers, when asked what they want to be when they grow up, said 'an influencer'.

But when we launched frank body in 2013, key opinion leaders (KOLs, as they were then known) were just emerging as a marketing channel. Instagram was still a new platform, and we were building our profile alongside these KOLs.

To start, we sent products to everyone we thought might have influence over our target demographic – think models, makeup artists, personal trainers, beauty journalists, actors or anyone in the health and wellness category.

Our strategy was entirely organic and relied on people liking the product. We would find the influencer on Instagram, slide into their DMs, ask if they'd like to get dirty with frank body, get their address and send the product. There was no contract, no payment and no obligation for them to post – but more often than not, they did.

Why? They wanted to be associated with our brand, they liked the product or they were hopeful we'd repost their content.

We always aimed for these partnerships to be mutually beneficial and enjoyable. Yes, we were charming, delightful and built real relationships via social media and email, but at the end of the day these were business relationships and we both had our own strategic objectives.

In our first year, our approach was volume. Get as much scrub out as we could. Our initial influencer list was 250 people, and we added to it every week. We would have sent over 1000 scrubs in our first year.

As we got bigger, we became more selective about who we worked with and began to pay influencers to create specific assets. Some of our early ambassadors like Tash Oakley, Tammy Hembrow and Steph Claire Smith now have millions of followers.

Over the years, we've seen it all – from paying a huge fitness influencer $15,000 for one Instagram post (only to realise her audience was predominantly males and bots after we made no conversions), to seeing an organic post by a micro-influencer double our monthly sales overnight. The world of influencers is constantly evolving.

One of the highest amounts we ever paid for an influencer was $250,000 for an American rapper. It was a flop. The goal was to break into the US market. The team ran all the numbers, did all the research. This was a big bet for us. The partnership included a feature in her video clip and two Instagram posts. There are a few reasons it flopped. We should have known it wasn't going well when she mispronounced the name of the product in the first video. But the main mistake we made was not having a strong relationship with the talent or the manager. After doing this for fifteen years, we can get an idea of whether a partnership is going to work after the first call. The best partnerships are when there's an immediate alignment. This relationship began as a battle and ended with us as the casualties.

Listen to your gut. Life is too short to work with arseholes.

Understanding the creator and curator economy

We hear a lot of talk about the creator economy and what it can do for brands. In reality, it's far more complex than giving someone your product to post about and making millions – at least, now it is. When we launched frank body, social media was somewhat simple, but before long the space became crowded, complex and commoditised very quickly. Social media is now a multilayered amplification system for brands. Even so, many businesses are stuck in the old way of doing things: engaging influencers and paying them in exchange for a post. The new social economy encompasses creators, curators and customers to reach as many eyeballs as possible, often more cost-effectively, helping with brand awareness and salience. Let's break it down.

The creator economy

The social media creator economy is a system where influencers and content creators engage with brands and audiences to create value.

Creators should be chosen based on brand alignment rather than just their follower count. Most creators perform best when they are given creative freedom to use their authentic voice.

Long-term partnerships tend to be more effective than one-off collaborations.

Compensation often works best with hybrid models that combine upfront fees and a performance incentive.

The curator economy

The social media curator economy is made up of individuals who specialise in collecting, organising and sharing valuable content or products for specific audiences. Unlike creators (who make original content), curators find and present the best existing content in organised, thematic ways. They often filter through massive amounts of content to surface quality material, adding value through thoughtful organisation and context.

These accounts build dedicated followings around specific niches or interests.

When crafting social media strategies for our clients, it's imperative we start with a blank canvas. What worked for one client at one point in time in a particular category will almost certainly not work for the next client.

At the ripe old ages of thirty-eight and thirty-nine at the time of writing this, we must be honest – we feel totally and completely disillusioned with social media. Most of the time. That is, until we come across a client willing to do the hard thing, the risky thing, the bold thing. Just like we did. The strike rate for this type of partnership is about one in one hundred. Most clients (bless their cotton socks) think they want the risky thing but are so hardwired to continue to do things the way it used to work, or in alignment with corporate values, that they simply can't gain any traction on social media.

How to Grow Your Audience

We can't convey social media strategy in a book: it will be outdated by the time you get to this page. What we can convey is a truth that will forever remain: you have to be willing to get out of your comfort zone for social media to work. Whether it's for your business or your personal brand, if you don't feel slightly uncomfortable, you're doing it wrong. Think of yourself as a giant cocktail shaker: one part excitement, one part nerves; shake vigorously and serve on ice. Don't hesitate. Order more.

Think about the advertisements that are burnt in your brain. Jingles that pop into your mind at 3am that you first heard in 1997. Hilarious skits that made you remember a business you wouldn't otherwise care about. Confronting conversations that stopped you in your tracks. No one ever remembers the ad that promotes every product attribute. Not even Apple do this, for all their focus on tech and product. At the core of it they are still utilising brand assets to appeal to a consumer's emotional desires through their content. More pixels equals better memories, for example.

Whether it be on social media or a billboard, having a point of view is the commonality. Pixel size does not discriminate.

A chat with Rachael Wilde – co-founder of tbh Skincare, Bouf and CMO at York St Brands

When it comes to growing a community of raving fans, Rachael is an expert. Her first brand, The Breakout Hack (formerly known as tbh Skincare) launched in 2020, when she was just twenty-three. Its debut product, the Spot Cream, offered a science-backed alternative to traditional acne solutions.

The brand gained immediate traction, generating $800,000 in revenue within eighteen months. Strategic retail partnerships with Priceline and Coles followed, putting the brand in more than 1200 stores across Australia. In 2025, they also launched into Boots in the UK.

In 2023, the brand merged with Boost Lab to form York St Brands, and Rachael stepped into the role of Chief Marketing Officer. The group went from a combined annual revenue of $5 million to $22 million the following financial year.

If that weren't enough, in 2025 Rachael engaged Willow & Blake to help create the brand identity for Bouf, a hair care brand targeting hair loss, with a smart yet chaotic energy. In its first week, Bouf achieved 5487 orders, sold more than 19,000 units, and generated more than $500,000 in revenue. Three weeks later, they sold out of their hero product, The Flouf Factor Growth Tonic.

Rachael's approach to marketing is raw, relatable and relentlessly community-first. It resonates deeply with consumers and has helped her brands stand out in a saturated market.

Here, she shares her thoughts on building a community of raving fans.

tbh Skincare is a brand built on community. Can you talk about who your community was when you started and how it's evolved?

When we started tbh, the community was very much organically built. It started with me organically posting from behind the scenes of the brand about how I was building it. I didn't have a following, but I was a heavy social media user. The community was people who were interested in that story and interested in the product offering – mid-twenties females interested in skin care who potentially had issues with acne, breakouts or misbehaving skin.

When we first launched, I focused on what was free, which was my time. I invested a lot of time in posting content and creating videos. I would do Q&As and Instagram stories every single week. There was always a mass of content going out from tbh. It's something that we've done from day one of the brand and that we still do now.

How did you grow your community? Where did you invest your marketing spend initially?

The initial marketing dollars went to influencer marketing and to Meta advertising. But with the iOS update that happened twelve months into our launch, Meta became quite an ineffective channel for us.

The community grew and evolved as we found new audiences through creators who were equally as passionate about the brand story. And then the second stage of growth for tbh beyond influencer partnerships was very much viral TikTok videos.

A good example of this is our Abbie Chatfield video. Abbie was behind our first viral moment. We worked with her shortly after she appeared on *The Bachelor*, when she was talking publicly about her acne challenges. A year later, she then talked about tbh organically on the radio. I filmed a TikTok of my reaction to hearing her rave about the product. I didn't think much of it – I filmed the content in my car, edited and posted, then closed TikTok. I woke up the next day and that video had gone viral. We ended up selling over 500 units just through that video. That was the moment I realised the power of content.

These days, we continue to post videos that go viral, achieving reach into the millions and sending a whole new community our way.

You are the queen of content. What advice do you have for founders on creating content that connects?

I've built our marketing team with content at the centre because I believe, without good content, you cannot market effectively. At the end of the day, everything comes down to content. You can get good media placement, great budgets – everything can be there, but without innovative, relatable, great content, you just don't cut through.

Firstly, what works will be specific to your brand. What works for us might not work for another brand.

I'll start with Boost Lab as an example. The audience is aged fifty plus, so they have better attention spans. They've got a little bit more time and they respond better to sponsored advertisements. But on social media, you aren't able to communicate a whole bunch of messages at once. So I asked, 'What's their biggest pain point? What's the one product out of the whole range they can understand in a one-minute video?' Just one – don't focus on the whole range. Then give them a reason to watch – you have to hook them in the first three seconds.

But also make sure it's realistic. Don't put a twenty-five-year-old in front of a fifty-year-old and get them talking about wrinkles and anti-ageing; it's just going to piss them off. Reflect the customer and the content, give them something realistic, something to relate to.

Keep it simple: one product, one benefit, how to use it. That's it.

Then it's about putting it in the right place, which for us was Facebook ads. This demographic is very responsive to Facebook ads with the right creator, which again was someone their age who they could relate to. Marrying up all those things was the way that we created wonderful content for Boost Lab that scaled really well. And when we got that formula right, it was the whole reason why their business boomed overnight.

We talk about formulas in our team all the time, in terms of a content formula that works for Boost Lab. There's a different content formula that works for tbh. If you're reading this, there will be a different content formula for your brand, too.

What's the formula for tbh?

For tbh, we had to throw everything at the wall to see what stuck. For every video that performs, you're gonna have 500 that flop, so get comfortable with failure. Consistency is everything. You have to relentlessly show up on these channels until you strike gold, and then you lean into that momentum. That's been the magic key for tbh.

It's a volatile place to be, TikTok – trends change all the time. You'll have something that performs one day that doesn't the next. You've got to keep trying new stuff. But when you see something that works, don't go back to the slick content plan that you had in place that you've spent time filming. Chuck it all in the bin and lean into whatever content at that point in time is working, because it's got an expiry date. When you've got an opportunity, you lean into it because it's like lightning in a bottle.

Having comfortability with failure, the consistency to show up again and again and the ironically trying approach of trying everything is what allowed us to find a content stream that worked for tbh. It was trend-led, slapstick humour and pranks. We hardly talked about the product.

What did you do differently when launching Bouf in 2025, compared to when you launched tbh in 2020?

We launched Bouf with a big bang. With tbh we were scrappy. In the early days when you're bootstrapping, you can afford to evolve over time. But we launched Bouf in a major way, going straight into retail. That's why we spent the time and money with Willow & Blake to ensure we had the brand and positioning right from day one.

We were really robust around how we built the brand, the brand label, the brand guidelines, the tone of voice – the whole structure around the brand was definitely nowhere near as established or well done when we were launching tbh. Together we worked out: who is this brand for? What does it look like? What does it sound like? How do we make sure we stand out? It had to be slick and perfect from day one.

We did that on the basis that we were expecting a fast start because we had bigger budgets and better resources this time around.

From a marketing perspective, we made our biggest ever marketing investment partnering with Indy Clinton as our face and ambassador to launch the brand. The deal is unique in that it was not your traditional post-for-pay relationship but an equity deal. We also worked closely with Hive HQ, who we have worked with for years on an intensive launch plan for earned media, earning organic coverage twice a day for the first seven days and a reach of over 13 million.

Yes, there were challenges, as there always are. But all the planning and investment paid off with us achieving 487 orders and over $500,000 in revenue in the first week. And in the first month, we sold out of our hero product The Flouf Factor Growth Tonic, which we had forecasted enough stock to last 6 months.

THE LESSON:

If you stand for nothing, you'll fall for anything. Don't jump on every trend. Building community means being consistently yourself.

Chapter 8

YOU CAN'T CONVERT DEMAND THAT DOESN'T EXIST: THE DEATH OF THE DTC DARLINGS

Of the direct-to-consumer (DTC) darlings from the 2010s, few are left standing.

Glossier, Warby Parker, Everlane, Casper, Allbirds ... we all rode the wave together wearing rose-coloured glasses as we disrupted our industries and made the most of the meteoric rise of social media and influencers.

Our phones were awash with shades of pink; voices felt human; products worked better (most of the time) – millennials (the consumers) ate up everything that millennials (the founders) served them. Everyone was hungry for something different – for brands that understood them, that saw them, that *were* them.

For a while, it was like printing money.

But then the machine stopped working.

You can pinpoint the beginning of the end for DTC brands to an exact date: 26 April 26 2021. This was the day that Apple rolled out iOS 14.5. Software updates generally don't destroy entire business models, but this one did. As part of a broader push for the tech giant to focus on privacy, the update required iPhone apps to give users the option to opt out of being tracked for advertising purposes. Apple's privacy changes meant we could no longer track campaigns end to end, and it became difficult to understand what was and wasn't working.

The algorithm changed overnight, making it almost impossible to replicate the results of the prior years.

Influencer costs went from three figures to seven figures in the space of twenty-four months.

The average cost of acquiring a customer through performance marketing grew by 222 per cent in the last ten years. 'In the US the cost to reach 1000 people on Facebook jumped from $6 to as much as $18,' a SimplicityDX study found.[4]

And rightly so – consumers have become more discerning with how they spend their money.

We are often asked, 'If you were starting today, what would you do?' To us this question is synonymous with, 'How would you revive a dying DTC brand?' The answer is the same: we would do everything differently now.

We've seen some pretty inferior 'analysis' (if one could call it that) about millennial brands from so-called brand strategists online. The arguments they make are weak at best, with no central theme other than to point out that millennial brands are outdated. Of course they are. Like anything, they are a product of their time and not indicative of how one would create a brand today – ten years later.

This book, with lessons from inside the machine, is designed to show you what went right and what went wrong, how timing is everything and why brand building is the most important metric for you to focus on. If you want to learn from the past to ensure a strong future for your brand, you need to finish this entire book.

To understand how a DTC/ecommerce brand was built in the 2020s and why you need to do things differently now, we need to first explore the roots of the DTC boom. It was defined by eight key features.

Key factors that drove initial growth

- Direct relationships with customers: You were not just another number to a millennial brand. The brands that succeeded invested in robust customer service teams, if it wasn't the founder doing it themselves. We replied to every email, every comment and built a UGC (user-generated content) strategy that made the big strategic companies quiver in their 54th floor, Central-Park-viewing boots.
- Innovative digital marketing strategies: Nothing will make you more innovative than having no money. When you can't rely on a $30 million campaign to make noise, you rely on your smarts; you rely on cutting through with a strong point of view; you rely on creating something shareable and worthy of talking about. The more money millennial brands had, the worse they became at innovative marketing.
- The rebirth of traditional industries: Warby Parker disrupted eyewear by cutting out middlemen and offering direct-to-consumer prescription glasses. Dollar Shave Club revolutionised razor sales by introducing subscription models to a stagnant industry. Casper challenged traditional mattress retail with online sales and home trials. All of them shook up industries that had established ways of doing things.

- Abundant venture capital funding: The money started flowing like a gutter after a storm. Often it was coming from venture capital or private equity that did not understand the brand and did not care about the customer – they only understood data points. This is why many investors drove the very brands they invested in into an early grave by pushing marketers to focus too heavily on metrics such as customer lifetime value. They forced brands to grow at the sacrifice of profitability, a lesson they would learn the hard way.

Marketing tactics that defined the era

- Social media: Most of the early DTC brands were launched without funding by first-time founders who saw the potential in the platform (Instagram) that they and all their friends were using. We knew what content we wanted and we curated aesthetically pleasing feeds for everyone else.
- Influencer partnerships: They were cheaper than any above-the-line campaign by a country mile, with fantastic reach and instant results that pleased every CEO and CFO. Many marketers received praise and treats, like dogs performing neat tricks.
- Subway/outdoor advertising campaigns: In the US specifically, this was a huge focus for DTC brands. It didn't necessarily sell products, but like planting a flag on the moon, it was a declaration that said, 'We are here.'
- Content marketing and storytelling: Millennial brands are defined by their desire to do things differently. In a body category that didn't stand for anything much, frank body stood for inclusivity, diversity and honesty – our customers were our story. Harry's *Five O'Clock* magazine was a digital publication focusing on men's grooming and lifestyle, curating content around masculinity and

self-care – something the incumbents in this industry had not done well.

The early brands were just that: early. Competition online was few and far between in the early years, but now we're competing in heavily saturated categories with bloated costs and exhausted customers. These days, the landscape is entirely different.

It shows us that timing is everything when it comes to success. The founders of the brands from the early DTC boom were in the right state of mind, with the right aptitude for risk. They were in the right place at the right time.

A Quick Walk Down Memory Lane: Revisiting Two DTC Darlings

Back in 2012, Michael Dubin released the first advertisement for his direct-to-consumer razor blade brand Dollar Shave Club, in which he pitched his product to consumers in a lo-fi piece to camera joking about overpriced razors and the hassle of buying them in physical stores.[5] It is still one of our favourite ads ever made. In 2016, Dubin sold his brand to Unilever for $1 billion.

By comparison, Casper launched in 2014 and quickly raised $340 million over five funding rounds, reaching a peak valuation of $1.1 billion in 2019. Casper's long-awaited IPO (initial public offering) in February 2020 was underwhelming, to say the least. CNN described it as 'officially a disaster'.[6] Casper's journey as a public company has been fraught with problems as they continued to haemorrhage cash even when the broader mattress market boomed during the pandemic.[7] Its stock price continued to decline until Casper decided to return to the private market in 2022, selling to consumer-focused private equity firm Durational

Capital Management for $6.90 per share, or just shy of $300 million (which you may notice is less than the total capital the company raised).

Even though the two companies were launched only twenty-four months apart, one on paper is a tale of success (for the founder); the other, by comparison to its peak valuation, a failure. So what happened?

There are many articles citing Casper's competitive landscape as the reason for its demise, but is that not also true of the razors category? Dollar Shave Club wasn't a lone wolf, happily removing facial hair without a competitor in sight. They were up against Gillette, Schick, Harry's and more. The idea that competition is the reason a company fails is lazy analysis at best.

Casper 'failed' for many more complex reasons:

- Unit economics: How anyone at Casper got a good night's sleep is beyond us. It has never been profitable, losing $92 million in 2018 and over $70 million in 2019.[8] Its economic earnings, the true cash flows of the business, declined from -$78 million in 2017 to -$95 million in 2018. Revenue grew 43% over the same time, as reported by Forbes.[9]
- Advertising spend: Casper pumps money into advertising. In 2017, the company spent 91 per cent of its gross profit on advertising. In 2018, Casper spent 80 per cent of its gross profit on advertising. In 2019, they spent 73 per cent of their gross profit on advertising. In 2020, they spent 60 per cent of their gross profit on advertising. This means that for every dollar Casper made off each mattress sale, 73 cents of that went back into Facebook, Spotify and Instagram ads.
    - Casper's revenue did not grow proportionately to its ad spend. Between 2017 and 2018, Casper grew its top line by 43 per cent; in 2018 and 2019, growth fell to 23 per cent; between 2019 and 2020, growth under COVID was an all-time low

of 18 per cent – which, at a time when we were all practically living in bed, seems to shows an epic lack of understanding of the customer.

- Poor planning: Casper's 100-night trial program also cost the GDP of a small nation – over $80 million in 2018 alone – because the mattresses cannot be reused after being returned.[10]
- The lack of repeat-purchase products: How many mattresses does one need?
- Values: The Casper brand didn't stand for anything. It's not the fact that there were at one point over 175 mattress-in-a-box companies, but rather that Casper's lack of differentiation ultimately meant there was no reason to choose them over any other questionably packed mattress. What did Casper stand for? We still don't know.

By comparison, let's explore what made Dollar Shave Club's exit successful and whether it was a good investment for Unilever.

- A strong launch: Dollar Shave Club had a launch campaign that dreams are made of. Dubin had no business experience to speak of, but what he had was far more valuable – he had human insight. His comedic improvisation skills mixed with his insight that men were fed up with the razors on offer led to the cult-status ad. Upon being uploaded to YouTube, the video received millions of views and shares, and within two days of its release the company received 12,000 orders.
- Accessibility: Dubin leveraged an existing category and instead of trying to educate customers about new technology, he simplified it for them, solving their pain points such as overpriced blades or running out of razors when they needed them most. By contrast, Casper may have appeared to simplify the purchase of a bed, but in reality they took away the most fundamental part of buying a

mattress: testing it out. (The $80 million in returns validates this flaw in their model.)

- Business model innovation: By shipping products direct to the door of the customer every month instead of having the customer head out to the shops, Dubin made things easier for them. He solved an actual problem they vocalised with the current offering. By 2016, Dollar Shave Club had 3.2 million subscribers.
- Profitability: It is rumoured that Dollar Shave Club never created any profit before it was bought by Unilever. Given that Dollar Shave Club was founded in 2011 and bought in 2016, that's a lot of years of losing money. It appears it was always trading on razor-thin margins (pun intended). Its expansion into grooming products never took off because their products were more expensive than the basics on offer at Boots or CVS.
- Acquisition: In 2016, Unilever brought Dollar Shave Club into its fold. The brand was Unilever's first razor brand and one of its earliest forays into DTC, serving as a testing ground. Unilever paid a billion dollars to buy 3.2 million subscription customers, which works out to $312 per customer. In today's landscape of sky-high customer acquisition costs (CAC), even if the brand has failed to scale adequately, this is actually quite reasonable CAC and provides a multitude of data points that Unilever could learn from.

The real winner here is obviously Dubin, who walked away with an unknown but presumably large amount of cash. The only difference between Casper and Dollar Shave Club? Timing. Dubin got out while the DTC sector was on fire. Casper hung on, clinging to the hope of an IPO that never thrived and no path to profitability.

The noise of the DTC boom reached a fever pitch during the pandemic and the collective finally decided: enough is enough. How many exclamation marks and time-sensitive deals can arrive in my inbox before I go on an unsubscribing spree? How many brands can one influencer promote before it all feels like one giant nonsensical and never-ending ad? It was too much noise. It was saying so much, without saying anything at all.

At the same time, the very investors that pushed brands to grow at any cost were realising that there was one cost they weren't willing to pay: their own winnings. They suddenly expected brands built on a strategy of 'grow, grow, grow' to pivot overnight to one of profitability (while still growing). That's like asking Charlotte Brontë to coach a basketball team – they require very different skills and it's hard to get the team on board. This is why we saw the sudden and catastrophic failure and collapse of so many brands. The rug was quite literally pulled out from under them; they ran out of cash and their valuations plummeted as investors changed their valuation methodology to more heavily focus on EBITDA (earnings before interest, taxes, depreciation and amortisation).

Now in 2025, with dozens of casualties in the feeds of our social media accounts and the weekly media reporting on another low-price buy out or collapse of a once unicorn-status business, what have brands and investors learned? Precisely nothing.

Brands continue to build poor business models. Investors don't allow for the natural growth of a business or acceptable levels of unprofitability or break-even periods at the start before achieving profitability. They now expect both, and expect them immediately.

Because of this pressure, brands continue to shout at customers, creating more products, creating more content, creating more emails, creating more, more, more. Consumers tune out because it becomes boring and annoying.

And because of this, the brands burn out their teams and they burn out their customers. The ultimate result is that brands build disconnected ecosystems of people, not communities, just like the stalwart brands did prior to the early DTC boom. We have come full circle.

The greatest lesson we can learn from the DTC darlings is that outside of your unit economics needing to stack up (more on that later), cultivating organic demand is crucial.

The idea that you can grow a business without demand for it goes against the core economic principles of supply and demand.

Many performance marketers will argue that you don't need to have brand recognition to scale in this day and age if you have strong product attributes because you can target customers through demographics, interests and psychographics online before they *know* about you. While that is true to an extent, our experience has shown that the tap eventually turns off. Performance marketing alone is not a long-term strategy for brand building and is often at odds with a profit and loss (P&L) report that shows profitability and strong repeat purchase rates. The logic that performance marketing is the key to growing a business is often propagated by people without a good understanding of the commercial realities of running a business, and how contribution margin per channel impacts the long-term business strategy. When you think about it practically, there is a saturation point at which performance marketing, because everyone is using it, simply cannot be profitable.

By comparison, unassisted brand recall – which can be simplified down to 'people searching for you online or reaching for you on a shelf because they know and remember you' – has far more long-term positive impacts for a business, especially on the P&L. However, most CMOs have a hard time getting their CFOs and CEOs to be patient enough to see the benefits of this approach. In times of economic uncertainty, brand spend is first on the chopping block, despite every recession teaching us that businesses who invest in brand building during that period almost always come out better off. And not just better off, but having experienced significant financial growth.

If no one wants the brand, there is no low-hanging fruit to gather up.

If no one wants the brand, there is no retailer to sell it into.

If no one wants the brand, there probably won't be a business in twelve months' time.

Demand is everything in marketing and if it's not there, you're dead in the water.

So how do we cultivate the ever-elusive demand and what impact does it have on metrics over time?

Let's explore.

There are some easy-to-access statistics online[11] that show the impact of brand building:

- Strong brands outperform the market by 134 per cent on average.
- Companies with strong brands see 20 per cent higher customer retention rates.
- Brand-led businesses achieve three times higher revenue growth compared to their competitors.
- Businesses with strong brands experience two to three times higher click-through rates on digital ads.
- Cost per acquisition (CPA) is typically 20 to 30 per cent lower for well-established brands.
- Brand awareness campaigns lead to 23 per cent higher conversion rates in performance marketing.
- Strong brands command 13 to 22 per cent price premiums over competitors.
- Brand-driven businesses recover three times faster from market downturns.
- Companies with strong brand recognition spend 50 per cent less on customer acquisition.

The Ehrenberg-Bass Institute has found that if a brand stops advertising, its sales will fall 16 per cent after one year and 25 per cent after two years.[12] This means you're at a serious disadvantage when a normal economic environment resumes.

A hundred years of data tells us that brands that advertise during an economic downturn grow, while brands that pull back end up in a worse position long term and struggle to recover.[13] This was first demonstrated in a study by Roland S Vaile in the recession of 1923,[14] and similar results have been found in studies ever since.

A study by MarketSense during the 1989 to 1991 recession found that brands that increased their advertising during this time saw serious sales growth.[15] Jif Peanut Butter and Kraft Salad Dressing brands saw growth of 57 per cent and 70 per cent respectively, while Pizza Hut sales rose 61 per cent. McDonald's slashed its sales budget and saw sales drop 28 per cent. The study's conclusion? The best strategy for surviving a recession is to get the balance right between long-term brand building and short-term sales promotion.

We do need to caveat here that a lot of the data in studies is from huge brands with hundred-million-dollar marketing budgets and omnichannel presence. For your average brand driving growth through TikTok, the data skews but does still ultimately show a strong correlation between awareness (with the right audience) and conversion. For example, a brand known by four out of ten consumers is 43 per cent more efficient in driving performance marketing outcomes on TikTok than a brand known by three out of ten consumers.

At the end of the day, a strong brand strategy comes down to having a consistent and future-focused approach to building a business. If you're in it for a quick buck, don't bother. If you're building a legacy, then you need to spend your time and energy on brand building ideally before, but if not, alongside your more tactical marketing efforts. That's what performance marketing is – a tactic several rungs down on the ladder of importance when developing a comprehensive marketing and brand strategy, let alone a business strategy.

For over fifteen years, we have created brand campaigns, performance campaigns, built and scaled businesses. In that time, we have seen again and again that the fundamentals of growing a strong business with good repeat revenue and a reasonable cost of acquisition is an investment in a unique and memorable brand, supported by clever and creative use of performance channels. It's not a theory, it's a fact.

So we summarised it into a nifty little saying: 'You can't convert demand that doesn't exist.'

Here are the metrics we are obsessive about tracking when it comes to brand demand.

Brand Awareness

Measures how familiar consumers are with a brand

Brand Perceptions

Examines the positive or negative attributes people associate with a brand

Brand Loyalty

Tracks the rate of repeat customers and their ongoing engagement

Brand Sentiment

Assesses consumer attitudes and feelings towards a brand

Brand Equity

Evaluates the overall value of a brand based on consumer perceptions and financial performance

Net Promoter Score

Measures customer satisfaction and the likelihood of customers recommending a brand to others

Purchase Intent

Indicates the likelihood that customers will buy a product or service

Share of Voice

Compares the level of brand mentions and conversations relative to competitors

Market Share

Represents a brand's percentage of total sales in an industry or market

Social Media Research

Tracks the number of people who see a brand's content on social media platforms

SEO Performance

Measures brand visibility in search engine results

Lessons from a Recovering Performance Marketer

It's not all doom and gloom. You can still achieve great things through performance marketing but it needs to be part of the strategy, not the strategy. We asked some of the best in the business about how to win at performance marketing without sacrificing brand.

Kate Howard and Emma Mulquiney – co-founders, Monday Digital

On winning with performance marketing

Kate and Emma are two of the smartest women we know. In 2024, they co-founded Monday Digital as an offering to better serve consumer brands in the ecommerce and performance marketing space and they also co-founded our business advisory, For Scale.

Kate Howard brings a distinctive approach that fuses brand building with performance marketing and consumer psychology. With over fifteen years of experience, she has developed a unique methodology that bridges these often-siloed disciplines.

Kate's expertise was honed as Head of Marketing at iconic Australian startups frank green and Sheet Society, where she played an instrumental role in their transformation from emerging brands to major global businesses. What sets Kate apart is her holistic view of marketing and her ability to tap into the customer's mindset. Kate understands that sustainable growth comes from strategies that deliver both immediate performance results and long-term brand equity.

Emma Mulquiney is a digital strategist with more than fifteen years of experience growing ecommerce brands across retail, wellness, and tech. She's held leadership positions driving digital strategy for startups and global brands including Nike, frank green, Sheet Society and Swisse.

Leading the ecommerce department at Monday Digital, Emma helps brands scale by combining data, creativity and smart execution. She has a deep understanding of online consumer behaviour and knows how to turn insights into results – whether it's optimising conversion rates, refining customer journeys or unlocking new revenue streams.

Emma's approach blends brand marketing with performance marketing, ensuring that digital growth isn't just about short-term wins but also about long-term brand impact. From A/B testing and forecasting to full-funnel strategy and channel optimisation, she builds ecommerce ecosystems that perform.

> 'To us, where we see businesses fall down with performance is when they lean so heavily into buying ads that they take their eye off the goal: building a strong standalone brand alongside a profitable product. We spend our days inside other people's businesses and there is a clear divide between the founders that understand the power of brand and their product, versus those that want to use performance channels to drive quick wins. For us, it's very clear: brand drives performance marketing. Performance cannot exist in a world without a brand. High-awareness brands get nearly three times the conversion of low-awareness brands. We know that if your brand is known by four out of ten customers, it will be 43 per cent more efficient in ad platforms (thanks to a recent TikTok and Tracksuit study). We need to break down the idea that it can be one without the other. It's like giving performance marketing

all the credit for the applause at a brilliant musical, when brand wrote the script, cast the show and sold the tickets.

Our top tip for winning on performance channels is to keep your brand and performance team together and operating as one. When these two functions divide and sit on opposite sides of the room, they don't create cohesive strategies. Performance strategy needs to sit incredibly close to your creative team.

Also, understand how you want your brand to show up across your performance channels and creatively strategise appropriately – don't expect what works on one channel to work on another. Put the effort into content strategies for each, and understand how your customers move across channels.

Finally – it is just as important to know what's working across every channel. It's easy to lean on performance channels that show quick results, but real brand growth comes from making sure every part of your marketing is pulling its weight. When you only look at one piece of the puzzle, you miss where the real wins are coming from. That means thinking about how email, organic, social, SEO, retention and paid all work together, not in silos. Assign KPIs and monthly targets across your entire marketing mix so that if your revenue result isn't where you need it to be, you're able to identify which channel isn't pulling its weight. So often we see performance channels being relied on to close gaps in business targets, without considering if there's a quick fix to underperformance in another area.

Some of the strongest results we've seen come from brands that treat every touchpoint as a revenue driver, not just the ones with the easiest tracking.'

Need more convincing?

Let's look at the data that supports brand building's impact on performance marketing and financial metrics.

Customer acquisition and retention

- According to McKinsey, strong brands see up to 20 per cent lower customer acquisition costs compared to competitors.[16]
- Brands with high recognition experience 15 to 25 per cent higher customer retention rates.[17]
- Companies with established brand presence see 2.3 times higher customer lifetime value.[18]

Performance marketing

- Performance marketing campaigns for well-known brands achieve 40 to 60 per cent higher return on ad spend.[19]
- Branded search terms convert at three to four times the rate of non-branded terms.[20]
- Social media engagement rates are 2.5 times higher for established brands.[21]

Financial and pricing impacts

- Strong brands command 15 to 25 per cent price premiums over generic alternatives.[22]
- Companies with high brand value show 1.5 to 2 times higher profit margins.[23]
- Brand investment leads to 30 per cent lower marketing costs over a three-year period.[24]

Long-term business benefits

- Businesses with strong brands are 60 per cent more likely to survive market downturns.[25]
- Well-established brands see 25 per cent higher employee retention rates.[26]
- Strong brands experience 40 per cent faster market penetration when launching new products.[27]

These metrics demonstrate that consistent brand investment creates a compound effect, improving both immediate marketing performance and long-term business sustainability. Brand isn't just fluff; it's a science that directly impacts a business's bottom line. The initial investment in brand building generates increasing returns through enhanced marketing efficiency, stronger customer relationships and improved business resilience over time – you have to have faith and stay the course to see these benefits.

Creating Strong Brands in Unexpected Places

Building a great brand in consumer goods categories is par for the course these days, but often where we see business owners go wrong they assume their somewhat traditional category can't be shaken up: think finance, law and HR. Often what is required in these categories that are usually dominated by tightly held and legacy incumbents is a drastically different approach to what has been done before, creating interest and generating demand where one can't compete on heritage, budget and the innate trustworthiness that comes with the old guard. Millennial and gen Z customers are increasingly turning to newer, more value-aligned offerings in traditional categories that not only meet the basic requirements of the service, but better understand who they are as customers. The brand aligns with the customer's view of themselves. Where we once became a customer of a bank because our parents opened an account for us when we were kids, we now actively seek out alternatives that provide not only better customer support and more flexible offerings, but a better feeling.

THE LESSON:

The right investments pay dividends.

Chapter 9

PRICING, POSITIONING AND PERCEPTION

Would you pay $3000 for a baby carrier?

How about $100,000 for a bag?

Or $1500 for a paper clip?

These are all pricing examples from real brands. Artipoppe, Hermès and Tiffany & Co. to be precise. How can they justify these prices? Brand.

The first luxury bag Bree bought was a Trapeze Bag by Céline. It was one of the quintessential 'it' bags of the early 2010s designed during Phoebe Philo's famous era now known as Old Céline.

It's quite a distinctive design: an architectural, almost sculptural structure with flaps that can fold in or jut out. The branding is very minimal and the colourways are all muted. Bree found a beautiful, smooth, navy and brown calfskin version in the Saint-Germain store in Paris. She'd seen the style all over Instagram on the arm of the models and fashion bloggers she followed. But she hadn't seen this colourway before. It was her birthday and she wanted to buy it for herself to mark some of the early success we were having at work. The experience was everything she imagined. Champagne in the store. A glamorous French sales assistant. She even took a cringe-worthy photo out the front with the bag still in the box.

The bag itself is lovely, but to Bree it was so much more than a bag – it was a ticket into a world she hadn't had access to before. A world of effortless refined French style. This was quiet luxury – the kind reserved for glamorous French bloggers. The price was higher than she'd ever paid for any item of clothing or accessory before, but that was the point. It was a statement that she could afford this lifestyle, even though she had previously never dreamed she could. Every time Bree wore that bag, she felt a little bit more powerful.

And that's the power of brand – a powerful brand made it possible for this a bag to represent so much more than a utilitarian object. And for a utilitarian object to command a price tag far beyond its use. Yes, Bree could have bought a much more practical version of that bag at a department store or a fake version of the Céline in Bali, but they would never give the same feeling.

Jean-Noël Kapferer and Vincent Bastien define the difference between 'premium' and 'luxury' like this: 'Premium means pay more, get more in functional benefits. Luxury is elsewhere: it signals the capacity of the buyer to transcend needs, functions, or objective benefits. This is how luxury brands are different from premium or super-premium brands: beyond the experience they bring creative power, heritage and social distinction.'[28]

Our strategy at frank body was definitely not to be a luxury brand like Céline. But still, we know people buy brands, not things and even 'masstige' or affordable products can and should be branded to appeal to one's sensibilities beyond function. People want to buy into something bigger than themselves, like a community, a feeling or a lifestyle.

Pricing is one of the often-overlooked areas of brand and marketing, but it's a key part of a customer's decision-making process. We have a saying that 'something is only worth what someone is willing to pay for it'. This is true for products and businesses. Pricing is much more than just a number on a spreadsheet – it talks to status, quality and dictates largely how much you can spend on marketing. To come up with your pricing strategy, you need to think about how much your customers will value your product and your brand.

Our original financial goals for frank body were to make enough money to cover our rent or to have extra beer money for the weekend. Our pricing strategy for the product was equally simple. Premium positioning, affordable price.

By using innovative, affordable packaging (aka kraft paper coffee bags as opposed to plastic tubs) and removing retailer costs, we were able to price our product at a significantly cheaper rate than most of our competitors.

Our Original Coffee Scrub was $14.95 with free shipping included. The way we managed to include free shipping was to send each scrub as a large letter, reducing our postage costs by ~80 per cent. It also meant we had to carefully squish each bag flat to ensure it fit through the slot of a post box. This simple hack saved us thousands of dollars.

We then piled on a tonne of premium social cues through our design and marketing, and social proof through influencer marketing and our customer-generated content.

Over the years, our pricing strategy has become a lot more sophisticated. It now takes into account all the line items that are required to get a product from a factory into a consumer's shower.

We've learned a lot about margins and how they can make or break a business, and we urge you to make sure you give yourself a healthy margin, no matter which category you are in. But in this chapter, we are going to explore different pricing strategies from a marketing perspective.

Perception

Perception is the way in which something is regarded, understood or interpreted.

Have you ever heard the saying, 'Dress for the job you want, not the job you have'? The same can apply to how you dress your brand.

From the day we launched, people have always perceived Willow & Blake to be a much bigger business than it is.

From the beginning, we set a standard for ourselves. From our website to our articles, our emails and our social media, we put effort into curating a brand.

It didn't matter if only ten people read the article or our Instagram post only got four likes – we knew we were building something. Slowly, 10 people becomes 100, which becomes 1000, which becomes 10,000, and so on.

If you're worried about trying too hard, you will never succeed. It's cool to care about what you are doing.

You decide how your brand will be perceived. Keep showing up as you want to be seen and eventually it will become a reality.

Pricing

We think we make rational choices. In truth, our brains are wired to seek shortcuts – like price – to help us decode value.

Different categories have different pricing strategies, but these six are the most common: luxury, masstige, value, penetration and skimming.

Luxury pricing

High prices carry lots of status, with no rational benefit for the high price. These brands are all about exclusivity – the high price is part of the allure, reinforcing the brand's positioning that says it's not for everyone.

Think: Louis Vuitton

Masstige pricing

Masstige ('mass' + 'prestige') pricing strikes a balance between accessibility and aspiration. It offers a taste of luxury at a more affordable price point, often through brand associations and partnerships or selective distribution.

Think: frank body

Value pricing

Value pricing focuses on delivering more for less – quality and utility at a competitive price. It appeals to practical consumers who weigh cost against benefits, not brand cachet.

Think: The Ordinary

Penetration pricing

Penetration pricing starts low to quickly attract customers, gain market share, or disrupt competitors. Once brand awareness grows, prices often increase gradually.

Think: Netflix (when they first launched)

Skimming pricing

Skimming sets prices high at launch to maximise profit from early adopters, then gradually lowers prices to reach broader segments. It's a common approach for innovative or first-to-market products.

Think: Apple.

How To Make Masstige Pricing Work

High volume

To make your affordable pricing model viable, focus on driving significant unit sales. This means prioritising distribution, accessibility and retail partnerships that could deliver scale. It also means keeping your audience relatively broad. The more expensive your products, the more niche your audience.

Bundles

Sell in step-by-step, daily or weekly routines; something your customer has to repeat and use multiple products for. Bundling products increases your average order value without compromising perceived affordability. Bundles also help you tell a story around usage, encouraging trial of multiple products at once. Tip: Always give three options; high, medium and low. People generally choose the middle option.

Offer lower-priced products (e.g. lip balms, minis)

We began making lip balms and minis as our gateway items for new customers. They introduced people to the brand and helped build brand familiarity fast. Beauty-to-go was a game changer for our business. Lip balms were great because they acted like mini billboards being carried around in public. Warning: Be careful with margins on minis.

Gifting

Holiday – the global celebratory period between November and January – is always huge for consumer brands. Think carefully about your pricing strategy. We strategically priced our holiday kits to cover everything from an under-$20 Kris Kringle through to a $50 special gift for a significant other. Key tip: People often shop to a specific budget per person at holiday time, so price in tiers that help them shop with ease.

Limited-edition products

Our limited scrubs often sold out. This created urgency and allowed us to test new product ideas without long-term commitment. They also gave us PR hooks and storytelling moments to re-engage loyal customers. Think about what products you can re-package as limited edition.

Repeat-purchase rates

Affordability was only one part of the equation – repurchase was the real driver of growth. We focused on delivering visible results and enjoyable user experiences to ensure customers came back. Make sure you track which products have a high repeat-purchase rate.

When Discounting Damages and When it Helps

This is a cautionary tale of the addictive nature of discounting.

Discounting is like gambling. You do it once or twice and win big. You see a huge pay-off. You feel great. The return is amazing. Everyone celebrates. But the more you do it, the lower returns become. You start to train your customer to expect you to discount. You look at other competitors and try to match their discounts. Then you go into retail and see their promotional schedule. Now your ecommerce business is competing with the physical retailers' discounts. Before you know it, you're one of those brands that is always on sale.

Discounting can either erode or enhance brand perception, depending on how and when it's used. Frequent or deep discounts can signal desperation, train customers to wait for sales, and undermine a brand's value, especially in premium or luxury categories where perceived exclusivity is key. On the other hand, strategic discounting – such as limited-time offers, loyalty rewards or end-of-season markdowns – can create urgency, drive volume and bring in new customers without damaging long-term brand equity. The difference lies in intent and execution: if discounts feel like a brand is devaluing itself, they weaken perception; if they feel like a considered reward or event, they can strengthen engagement and loyalty.

Finding the right balance with discounting comes down to aligning your pricing tactics with your brand positioning and customer expectations.

Here's how to strike that balance:

- Start with your brand role: If you're a luxury or premium brand, discounting should be rare, controlled and framed around exclusivity (such as private sales or loyalty access). For value or masstige brands, promotions can be more frequent but still need structure to avoid brand fatigue.

- Use discounting as a tool, not a crutch: Discounting should support specific objectives – clearing end-of-line stock, acquiring new customers, or boosting short-term volume – not patch poor sales or weak marketing.
- Preserve perceived value: Always make the *why* clear – tie it to an event, milestone or season. 'Because we're desperate' is never a good message, even if it's unspoken.
- Protect your core pricing: Even during a sale, ensure your full price remains the reference point. This helps customers still believe the product is worth its original value.
- Reward loyalty, not laziness: Consider offers that feel like rewards – bundles, early access, or gifts with purchase – rather than blanket markdowns that devalue your entire range.
- Consider alternatives: Gifts with purchase, free express shipping, extra loyalty points, charity donations and custom merch are all other alternatives to traditional discounting. Think about what other levers you can pull.

Ultimately, the right balance is when discounting drives short-term growth without rewriting how people perceive your brand in the long run.

Advice for those brands stuck in a sales cycle

We like to think of things in the long term and the short term. Every business has a long-term goal. Maybe it's an exit. Maybe it's a build to step back. Maybe you want your children to take it over. To do that, the business still needs to be there and be worth something in ten years' time. And to build the equity of a brand that is still standing in ten years (particularly if you would like to have that brand acquired), you need to do the activity now to build the brand. That same brand-building activity is what will attract a customer's attention, creating mental availability for you. And when we talk brand building, we're not talking old-school through-the-line campaigns – the way we engage with brands has changed. We want personal, clever moments with brands.

Every time we run a promo, we devalue the long-term brand equity we are trying to build. We are self-sabotaging for a moment of short-term gratification. Granted, some businesses need to do this to support cash flow and keep the lights on, but a lot of brands have simply got into the habit of short-term marketing driven by performance marketing and promotional schedules where they can see the return straight away.

If you plant seeds in a garden, you don't expect to walk out the next day and see flowers. It takes time. We nurture the garden, tend to it, fertilise it, water it and over time, we see the flowers bloom. Brand building and retraining customers out of promo shopping is exactly the same – both are exercises in patience.

You need to think of it as not just repositioning the price and the product, but the brand and how people perceive it. How can you create value for customers in other ways?

Practically, start with a data dive: find out who shops full price, when, what, where and why – then build your marketing plans around acquiring more of that customer archetype.

Giveaways and competitions: A sale alternative

What do you do with a bathtub full of thousands of old body balms? You run a giant version of 'guess how many jelly beans are in the jar'.

Due to a manufacturer's printing error, we had a bathtub filled with thousands of unsellable body balms in our office. We hated the idea of sending them to landfill and instead used them as an art installation and adopted a 'free to good home' policy for anyone who visited. One day we had the idea to run a competition to guess how many balms were actually in the bathtub. We put the post up with a simple incentive of a $150 voucher and it went nuts. Over 9000 comments – our highest post engagement to date.

But then we had a scary realisation: to run this competition legally, we had to know the exact answer. Cut to the whole team sorting thousands of balms into piles. It took us a long time, but we got there. The answer? 5455 body balms.

The lesson? Sometimes the simplest competitions are the best. And really consider the logistics when it comes to running competitions.

Giveaways and competitions have long been a marketer's secret weapon. They drive brand awareness, fuel customer acquisition and generate serious hype without touching your price point. When done right, they tap into our primal urge to win. People start acting irrationally. They buy more, share more, sign up faster and stick around longer. All for the chance at something that feels just out of reach.

There's logic to the madness. A well-timed competition creates a sense of urgency and exclusivity. It gives people a reason to act now and talk about it while they do.

At frank body and Willow & Blake, we've run competitions of all shapes and sizes for clients and our own brands. They continue to be a solid tactic for growth if they're done well.

Two ways to play: Games of chance versus games of skill

There are two primary mechanics to choose from when running a competition:

Games of chance

These rely on luck and are designed to be fast, simple and scalable. They're especially effective for top-of-funnel campaigns or product-led growth.

- Buy to enter: *Buy any product to go in the draw to win.*
- Tag to enter: *Tag a friend to go in the draw to win.*
- Sign up to enter: *Join our email list for your chance to win.*

Great for: sales spikes, list-building and social engagement.

Games of skill

These require participants to do more than just show up. They're judged on creativity, originality or accuracy and often result in richer content or deeper engagement.

- Answer in fifty words or less: *Tell us why you deserve to win.*
- User-generated content: *Send us your best selfie with our product.*
- Classic guessing games: *How many lip balms are in the jar? Closest answer wins.*

Great for: content generation, community building and boosting engagement rates.

Case Studies: Competitions

We've run dozens of giveaways; some big, some scrappy. Here are three of the most impactful:

The golden frank

Inspired by *Charlie and the Chocolate Factory*, this campaign was as simple as it was effective. During the month of June, anyone who purchased a frank body scrub had a chance of receiving theirs in a gold foil pouch. Inside: a ticket to Bali.

The concept was fun, nostalgic and created a genuine moment of surprise. We ran it for three consecutive years and every time, monthly sales increased between 24 and 34 per cent.

Key takeaway: Don't underestimate the power of storytelling and a juicy price. When the reward is tangible and well aligned, people keep coming back for more.

Hotel Pink

To launch our loyalty program Hotel Pink, we offered one lucky winner and their bestie a stay at a real-life 'Hotel Pink': The Royal Hawaiian in Waikiki. To generate buzz, we flew five influencers (and their plus-ones) to Hawaii to document the experience in real time while the competition was running.

In the first week alone, over 2500 people signed up to the loyalty program. The campaign turned a program launch into a dream experience and gave our community a clear reason to get involved early.

Key takeaway: Your campaign should make the prize *feel* attainable but aspirational. And if you can create FOMO in real time, even better.

Shimmer Scrub referral drop

This campaign was all about pre-launch hype. To build the waitlist for our limited-edition Shimmer Scrub, we created a tiered referral system:

- Refer three friends → Custom merch stickers.
- Refer ten friends → Free Shimmer Scrub.
- Refer 20 friends → Custom frank body denim jacket.

The campaign caught fire. It resulted in over 50,000 people signing up to the waitlist – giving us a warm, engaged audience to launch to.

Key takeaway: People love exclusivity. Make your reward feel like a backstage pass, and they'll work for it – especially when it involves community, collectability or personal status.

Escape the Everyday

In 2023, we launched a sub-brand, Everyday by frank body. Why? Because we needed to create an offering that was suitable for mass channels such as supermarkets and pharmacies. To celebrate our launch into Coles we ran a competition called 'Escape the Everyday' with Luxury Escapes. This involved putting little neckties promoting the competition on all of our Body Wash bottles. It was a clever way to advertise and boost sales without paying the expensive grocery point of sale advertising prices. The competition again was simply this: buy any Everyday by frank body Body Wash, enter your proof of purchase and go in the draw to win a holiday with Luxury Escapes. We had over 2000 entries and a 13 per cent increase in Everyday orders.

Would we run these again?

Not all competitions age well. Some of these ideas we'd approach differently today; refining the mechanics, rethinking the incentives or aligning the prizes more closely with values like sustainability and inclusivity. But the underlying principle still holds:

- Make the reward desirable (but brand-aligned). Think about what your customers want but maybe wouldn't buy for themselves.

- Make the entry mechanism simple (but not boring). Don't get too complicated or fancy.
- Create a moment your audience wants to talk about. Word of mouth is key.

When people want to win, they want to belong. And when they want to belong, they engage – again and again.

Beyond Price and Positioning: Why You Need to Know *All* of Your Numbers

In the early days of Jess's career, she self-sabotaged by saying she wasn't a numbers person. The truth was, she just didn't find knowing the numbers and detail as interesting as the creative aspects of her job. She quickly found out the hard way that was a very silly way to run a business. She made a huge effort to improve her understanding of the fundamentals and in time, over many years, grew her capabilities to that of a seasoned CMO and then finally took that job on with the seriousness it deserved. But it took a lot of effort and a lot of time building giant Excel spreadsheets that would span multiple departments and regions, so that she could make smart decisions about product pricing and positioning. Any creative marketer who wants to develop a comprehensive brand and marketing strategy needs to understand their numbers in totality. If you don't, then we're sorry you tell you, but you're not really doing the work of a strategist or CMO. You're cosplaying. You need to get good at numbers, even if you define yourself as creative. Stop delaying the boring stuff and soon enough you'll find yourself making the best decisions of your life and having conversations about the business with ease and confidence.

To develop a suitable price and positioning strategy, you also need to develop a smart total numbers strategy that factors in every aspect of

In the first few months of frank body, in 2013, our corridors looked like this as we packed and mailed every package ourselves.

Building a brand on a budget meant using the fancy toilets at a local cafe to shoot product images, 2013.

Co-founders of frank body in 2013 on a 'Directors' Retreat' to plan the next phase of growth and test product samples: (L–R) Steve Rowley, Erika Geraerts, Alex Boffa, Jessica Hatzis.

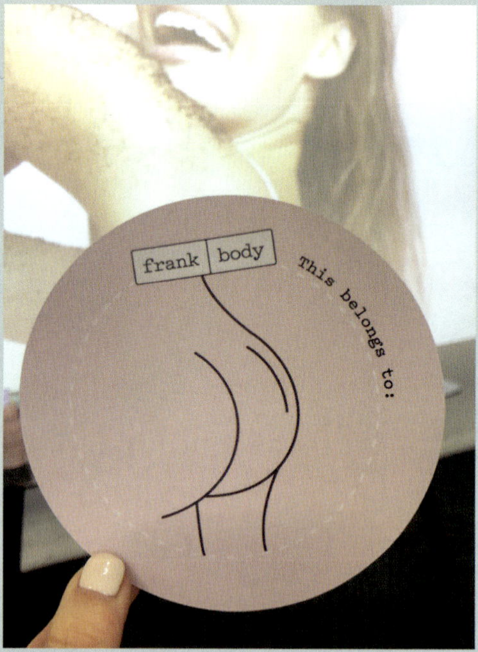

Some of the merch that frank body designed in 2014 for brand activations – a nod to our coffee-based roots, and, as always, a bum icon.

Bree Johnson (left), and Jessica Hatzis and Bree Johnson (right), with youthful naivety and friendship on our side back in 2015.

Willow & Blake HQ, circa 2016. Everyone in the neighbourhood thought our fancy office was a coffee shop and kept wandering into it in search of a long black. Alas, we had a different coffee-based product on our minds.

Co-founders of frank body in 2016, on set for our first major brand campaign: (L–R) Bree Johnson, Steve Rowley, Jessica Hatzis, Alex Boffa.

The frank body team in the UK in 2016, when we landed deals with Boots and Liberty: (L–R) Jessica Hatzis, Bree Johnson, Steve Rowley, Alex Boffa.

Our launch into MECCA stores across Australia in 2016 – naturally, we took over the windows.

Our first pop-up to celebrate the brand's fifth birthday, conceived and built in a matter of weeks, with lines around the block.

Bree Johnson (left) and Jessica Hatzis (right) in 2015 and 2017, respectively: twenty years of friendship and business.

Our first American office in Soho, New York, after a bi-coastal search for our US home. Our team of six worked here from 2017 to 2020, overseeing US and Canadian expansion.

Winning the Veuve Clicquot New Generation award in 2017. This was followed by a trip to France, where we got to christen our vines by pouring champagne on them. It was fun. Life is less bougie now, with four kids in the mix.

Winning Cosmopolitan's
Women of the Year Award
in 2017.

Jessica Hatzis and Bree Johnson in 2023. Jess was six months pregnant and running out of breath on the podcast tour.

Jessica Hatzis shot by Kate Shanasy in the frank body and Willow & Blake HQ in 2023.

Bree Johnson on Mark Bouris's podcast in 2023.

the business in order to maintain a healthy margin when all is said and done. This means you should never jump to plucking a price out of thin air, but rather do the very methodical and sometimes lengthy process of building out a proper budget.

Know thy unit economics

You should know the following numbers like the back of your hand:

- product cost
- packaging cost
- shipping cost
- average order value
- customer acquisition cost
- gross margin per unit.

If you don't have the answer to all of these, do not spend another cent on marketing until you do.

Growth versus profitability

The age-old question is which to sacrifice – growth or profitability. However, we'd like to offer you an alternative solution to slow down and achieve both outcomes simultaneously. Get into the weeds of your data and numbers so that you can leverage smart decisions that make growth and profitability best friends.

Calculate your monthly burn rate

'Monthly burn rate' refers to how much money a brand is losing each month to operate its business. It's calculated by subtracting total monthly expenses (including costs like payroll, marketing, rent, inventory and operations) from monthly revenue. For example, if a brand spends $500,000 monthly but only generates $300,000 in revenue, its burn rate would be $200,000 per month. When you're starting out, it's normal for your expenses to be higher than your revenue, but you need to draw a line in the sand where you cut costs if you haven't been able to outpace your expenses with your sales.

Set a customer acquisition cost (CAC) ceiling

You need to do this to ensure your marketing efforts are worthwhile, particularly across performance marketing. However, do not confuse the idea of maintaining a healthy CAC with not investing in brand building. Brand building will reduce your CAC in the long term if you review your data points for both brand and performance accurately. This is often where brands (and their leaders) go wrong, so we will deep dive into this concept later.

Setting a CAC ceiling happens in four steps:

1. Calculate customer lifetime value (LTV):
    - Multiply average order value by purchase frequency.
    - Multiply by average customer lifespan.
    - Subtract cost of goods sold and servicing costs.

2. Apply the LTV:CAC ratio rule:
    - Maintain a minimum 3:1 ratio of LTV to CAC.
    - Example: If LTV is $300, CAC ceiling should be $100.

3. Consider your margins:
    - CAC should not exceed 30 per cent of your first-year customer revenue.
    - Factor in overhead costs and desired profit margins.

4. Account for payback period:
    - Set your CAC ceiling to allow payback within a timeframe that is suitable to your product lifecycle and average LTV.
    - Calculate monthly customer revenue to determine feasible acquisition spend.

Define target profit margins

You need to know what you're chasing for clarity within an organisation. 'Profitability' could be one dollar in the black, or one million dollars in the black. Therein lies the problem with using loose terminology and not having enough specificity with our goals.

Set specific goals using these steps:

1. Study your competitors
    - Research industry-standard margins for your category.
    - Compare margins of successful competitors.
    - Account for business model differences (DTC versus retail).

2. Understand your cost structure breakdown
    - Use the table below to work through your key financials.

Margin Type	Target Range	Key Considerations
Gross Margin	60–80%	Product costs, shipping, packaging
Operating Margin	15–30%	Marketing, overhead, labour
Net Margin	10–20%	After all expenses and taxes

Set your gross margin targets

A lot of people will tell you the more expensive the brand, the higher you should set your gross margin (GM) targets. In our experience, the opposite is true. Low-price-point brands are already dealing with slim margins and should be the most discerning when it comes to setting high GM targets. We would aim for a minimum of 55 per cent no matter what the price point, but this number should ideally sit in the mid-60– 75 per cent range.

Establish sustainable growth rate goals

Spikes in growth can be exciting, but also extremely destabilising for a brand: you run through inventory, you have lulls, you over-forecast based on non-repeatable events. We don't love sales for this reason. We prefer slower, more predictable revenues that allow us to forecast and plan accurately. It doesn't mean we're not ambitious, but in order to have an entire organisation on board with your goals they need to believe those goals can be achieved and achieved well. Here's how you can do that:

1. Set realistic targets
    - Monitor and optimise unit economics before pursuing aggressive growth.
    - Consider available capital and runway requirements. Don't drive your business into a cash flow crisis for the sake of growth.
    - Look at your history – it's a telling story of what is to come.

2. Track key metrics
    - Customer lifetime value (LTV) to ensure sustainable growth. Remember that it is important to understand, but it is NOT the be-all and end-all that investors would have you think it is, especially for omnichannel brands.
    - Monthly burn rate and cash flow management.

   - Customer acquisition costs relative to revenue.
   - Investment in brand building. In particular, ensure that you're not under-investing and expecting performance to do the heavy lifting.

3. Use an implementation framework
   - Set specific financial metrics for tracking progress.
   - Develop pricing strategies that support growth goals.
   - Monitor and adjust based on market conditions and performance data.

Remember that sustainable growth is more important than rapid expansion. Many widely recognised consumer brands struggled precisely because they prioritised growth over sustainable unit economics.

THE LESSON:

Eventually, ignoring the boring bits of brand and business will kill you more than learning how to use Excel.

A chat with sisters Daniella Dionyssiou and Natalia Suesskow, the co-founders of VRG GRL

VRG GRL is an iconic Australian fashion brand founded by sisters Daniella Dionyssiou and Natalia Suesskow in 2007. Their story is one of family, creativity, resilience and evolution.

Like people, brands grow. Daniella and Natalia understand that evolution isn't just inevitable, it's essential.

They were just seventeen and nineteen when they opened a small store in Brisbane's Elizabeth Arcade. From day one, they found their customer by offering something no one else could: their point of view. Early VRG GRL was a curated mix of emerging labels, vintage pieces and a small collection of kimonos designed by the sisters themselves – a clear signal of what was to come.

Today, VRG GRL is a multimillion-dollar global ecommerce brand that designs and creates clothes. The business now exclusively stocks its own label, with every piece dreamed up in-house and bearing the unmistakable fingerprints of its founders. Design, fit and detail are obsessively refined.

Known for its effortless edge and cult following, VRG GRL doesn't follow fashion cycles, it follows conviction.

We spoke with Daniella and Natalia about defining their position, staying true to their creative instincts, and what the future holds for the brand.

Who is the VRG GRL customer today, and how has she evolved since the brand's early years?

Dan & Nat: The customer has grown up as we have. Our demographic of customers was always really young, and since we did our full re-brand a few years ago she has grown up as the brand has.

VRG GRL has often been mislabelled as a 'fast fashion' brand. How has the brand actively tried to shift such perceptions?

Dan & Nat: Behind the scenes we have done a lot of work to position VRG GRL where we want the brand to be sitting, designing every piece in-house and having complete control over all factories we work with. Making sure they have certifications is a big, important part. Lengthening our lead times and design processes has also helped with this, and the journey of getting B Corp certified has made us aware of what else we can do to be constantly improving. Willow & Blake have helped with this by bringing all the hard work we have done over the years together to create a clear brand guide and tone of voice.

What does the creative process look like at VRG GRL and why is it important to bring everything under one roof?

Dan & Nat: The creative process at VRG GRL is one that is constantly changing, evolving, innovating. We are always looking forward and never back.

Your tagline 'It's better on the edge' captures VRG GRL's philosophy perfectly. What does 'the edge' represent to your team and the brand?

Dan & Nat: This tagline for us sums up the true essence of the brand, which is that we like to push boundaries. We like to always be on the edge with everything we do, as in never boring, never playing it too safe.

Tell us about how refreshing the brand's voice shifted things for your team internally.

Dan & Nat: It was great to put on paper what was in our heads, and get this across to our wider team in a clear way. Sometimes, as founders who are heavily involved in different aspects of the business, it can be hard to get our thought process across to our wider team.

Talk to us about the importance of pairing messaging with the brand's visual identity.

Dan & Nat: For us, the brand's visual identity was easier to get consistent, but consistent messaging and tone of voice was something that was hard to have all team members aligned with. The brand voice and visuals need to go hand in hand, and the visual identity is much more cohesive with the tone of voice in line as well.

Looking back at VRG GRL's journey so far, what's a milestone or moment that feels especially defining for you?

Dan & Nat: We don't really have a defining moment or milestone. I think, for us, having years of work with the rebrand finally coming into fruition is something that is really nice to see.

What's next for VRG GRL? Where do you want to take the label from here?

Dan & Nat: For us, the future is so exciting. We are in a growth stage. We are opening a few physical stores in the near future, hoping to become B Corp certified early next year, always evolving and innovating.

Do you have any advice for founders or brand teams looking to undertake a brand repositioning or rebrand?

Dan & Nat: Our advice would probably be that it takes a lot of work before you see the impact. You have to be prepared to sometimes take a step back to take steps forward and grow. For us, it's taken years of consistency and work to rebrand and reposition VRG GRL before we have actually seen it come to fruition.

Chapter 10

BIG BAD COPYCATS

The first time we saw a copy of a brand we had created at Willow & Blake, we were heartbroken. By the time we launched our own brand, we were almost used to it, but it was still frightening. Fear took over. We remember thinking it was all over. Done, dusted, thanks for playing. Then we saw another and another. And another. Eventually, we realised this was inevitable and perhaps even flattering. Instead of worrying, we stopped looking in the rear-view mirror. We knew that someone would always be tailgating us – we had to outpace them and outwit them at every single turn. It became our superpower. This is why authentic brand building is so important.

Sit Down, It's Story Time

It's 2015. We're on track for $20 million in revenue purely from frankbody.com. We have eight SKUs. We're gaining traction globally and attracting the attention of big celebrities and media. We lead a team of fifteen across the two businesses. Willow & Blake is growing quickly at the same time. We sign on lululemon and Lee Jeans as clients. We hire an Account Manager and a Personal Assistant to stop our heads from imploding.

We've upgraded from our humble studio with no heating and chairs that gave us ongoing back issues to a two-storey office with proper ergonomic office chairs. We have a boardroom with space for twenty people where we regularly hold (slightly dysfunctional) family lunches and (even more dysfunctional) all-hands meetings. The kitchen, however, is still connected to the bathrooms in the most unsanitary of setups to ever exist.

There's a green clawfoot bathtub in the corner filled with frank body balms salvaged from a renovation at Jess's parents' place. A pink neon 'f' is nestled among a jungle's worth of plants that we will continually kill and replace over the next few years. We're still in the startup phase where we can go rogue, which means we haven't progressed to systems and processes yet. Jess, Eri and Bree sit in an area called 'the Vagina Club' at the top of the stairs. There's no door, but entering is a little like walking into a lioness's den. There's a fluffy cloud-shaped rug on the floor that Jess likes to sit on and write. The boys have their own room dubbed 'the Boys' Club.' How 2015 of them.

On Fridays, our office manager puts out the most delicious cheese platters and we drink bottles and bottles of wine.

Our days are busy. They are now filled with all the normal responsibilities of running our two businesses, but on top of that we have interviews, press trips, talks, meetings and a lot of HR. One thing no one tells you about being the boss is that managing people will start to consume your entire day, leaving you with the hours between 5pm and midnight to do your actual work. You're no longer in control of your calendar as it's filled with putting out fires and making sure everyone else is on top of their work. But despite the chaos and fatigue, we're in the thick of something exciting and all-consuming. We know we're onto something special – although, deep down, we're not quite sure how long it will last.

In September 2024, our PR manager comes running up the stairs into our lair. 'Have you checked Slack?' she asks. We glance up from a rare moment of actual strategic work with quizzical looks. Recently we've dubbed Slack 'the Devil', so we've been muting channels and going offline to ensure we can do our jobs.

We pull up the PR channel at her request and see a link to a video interview with Ariana Grande by *Elle* Japan. 'Go to the four minute fifteen second mark. She's talking about frank.'

We hit the link and there it is: Ariana is sitting in a simple studio, her signature Bambi eyelashes are thick and black, she has a high ponytail and her long brunette locks cascade down around her shoulders.

The question is in Japanese, but we manage to translate it roughly as, 'What's your favourite skincare product?'

Ariana answers: 'My favourite body product at the moment is called frank body scrub and it's all vegan, not tested on animals. It's made of coffee beans and coconut and all yummy goodness, and I love that it's not tested on animals.'[29]

A picture of our humble coffee scrub fills the YouTube screen. We all scream.

Ariana Grande, one of the biggest pop stars in the world, is raving about our product. We are elated. We take this footage and run with it. We plaster her review all over our social media, write blogs about it, tell the media, put it in pitch decks, put it on our website. Her fans also start to share the news and come across our website. For a small brand from Australia, the organic endorsement from a big US celebrity is a game changer. We've had organic celebrity endorsements before – Jessie J posted about frank body on her Instagram. Kourtney Kardashian posted a photo with our scrub on her bathroom shelf. But this interview with

Ariana is totally unique because she's talking about how the product aligns with her values. This shows she not only loves the product, but she's taken the time to read the back of the pack and knows the brand stands for more than just smooth skin.

Ariana Grande's fan base is a perfect match for our brand. They're young, very values-driven and highly attuned to what their favourite pop star recommends. Ariana says 'Jump', they say 'How high?' Two of the biggest drivers for consumers aged sixteen to twenty-four are social proof and value alignment, which means Ariana's audience become part of the frank body community – first, because their idol Ariana told them to, but then (more importantly) they stay because our brand speaks to them.

We obviously waste no time sending Ariana more product and start to build what we believe to be a good relationship with her manager. Spoiler alert: we're wrong.

Twelve months later, Ariana Grande launches her own coffee scrub into Ulta, one of the biggest beauty retailers in the US. This is the same retailer we've been pitching to.

Our world comes crashing down. This is the end, we say. We knew it was too good to be true. Ulta was our major US retail play and even though we've always prided ourselves on our speed, we've been beaten at our own game.

We're angry. Over the last year there have been too many copycats to keep track.

Boss Bitch Coffee

Mr Bean Coffee

Body Blendz

Bare Bar

Sportsgirl and Target even launched their own coffee scrubs.

A company in Russia ripped off our whole website including the source code.

Our once-unique product is now available everywhere, for cheaper – but Ariana's is the one we are most worried about. A celebrity founder and a huge US retailer. What will this do for our US plans?

At first, we want to fight them. To do something. Make them stop. We call lawyers and get ready for battle.

The sad news is, there's nothing we can do. At this point in time, we don't have a patent and Ariana isn't breaching trademark or IP (intellectual property) laws.

There are generally three types of IP infringements that can occur:

- Trademark infringement: This involves using a trademark (like a logo or brand name) that is confusingly similar to a registered trademark without permission, potentially leading to consumer confusion and damage to the original brand's reputation.
- Copyright infringement: This occurs when someone copies, distributes or uses a copyrighted work (like a song, book or software) without the copyright holder's permission.
- Patent infringement: This happens when someone makes, uses or sells an invention that is covered by a patent, without the patent holder's permission.

We learned a lot from that 2015 debacle.

Even though our copycats were using similar recipes and brand codes like the same fonts and colours, the differences were enough to not mislead the consumers.

Our anger turned to frustration. We became obsessed with watching what these copycats were doing and trying to predict their next moves. We would screenshot and send each other social posts they'd copied from us at all hours of the night. The obsession became unhealthy. We tried some of their products and confirmed they weren't even close to the same high quality we offered our customers – they were clearly in it for a quick buck.

But we still felt hard done by. And most importantly, we kept wasting time, energy and money being angry at the copycats.

Eventually we had a founder meeting to decide our course of action. We decided we had to stop wasting our energy on them. That didn't affect them at all. In fact, all it did was use up the precious time we had to grow our brand. They had no idea we were sitting behind our screens fuming – and if they did, they didn't care. Technically they hadn't done anything wrong. We finally realised that if we couldn't stop them from copying us, we had to evolve.

We decided to use that energy to innovate and progress. We decided these were our last days being a 'scrub brand' and it was time to become a full body and skincare brand.

We went straight to our customers to ask if they were interested and what they wanted us to make. The response was overwhelming – yes, they wanted other products. The most requested item was a moisturiser to follow the body scrub or to be used on alternative days to the body scrubs.

This led to us making our very first non-scrub product, a caffeinated body balm. This product was 98 per cent natural, spiked with green coffee bean extract and housed in a beautiful almond oil base to complement the Original Coffee Scrub. It targeted the same skin conditions as the OG scrub and was an instant success. We sold both products as a kit and increased our average basket size by 30 per cent. Here we learned an important lesson about the power of routines.

Step 1: Scrub.

Step 2: Rub.

It was simple, and that's what our customers wanted. It went bananas.

From here, we didn't slow down. The next most requested product was a face scrub. Many of our customers were using the body scrub on their faces, which it wasn't designed for. Taking the key learning from the body kit, we decided to launch a three-step face routine.

Step 1: Cleanse with our caffeinated charcoal cleanser.

Step 2: Scrub with a creamy face scrub.

Step 3: Moisturise with our everyday caffeinated moisturiser.

Despite being called 'frank body', the face products also landed with customers straight away. The face kit and the individual creamy face scrub became some of our most successful products of all time. The face scrub is still available, kicking goals and smoothing faces today.

At the time of writing, we have over thirty SKUs across five 'stories' – which are essentially the themes we use to categorise our products. Our range spans body scrubs, body washes, lip balms, face masks, moisturisers and serums. The Original Coffee Scrub remained our bestseller for eight years until it was eventually knocked off the top spot by our Glycolic Body Scrub, an acid-based acne-fighting body scrub which ushered in a new era for the brand where we transitioned from coffee-based products to high-performance products with more sophisticated ingredients.

And those copycats? None of them exist today in any significant way. If you google 'Ariana Grande coffee scrub', you can buy some on eBay, but its stint in Ulta was short.

Our Top Tips on How to Deal with Copycats

Decide what's an actual infringement

Everyone has ideas – execution is everything. Being first to market is not always key. Being first to scale is.

Imagine this: you've had an idea for a product. There's nothing else like it. You spend months thinking about it, then you start working on it. A year later, you open your Instagram and see someone has just launched the same idea.

This happens all the time. No, they didn't steal your idea. Even if they were inspired by you, there is nothing legal stopping them from launching their brand unless your product is patented. If someone has infringed on your trademark, copyright or patent then it's time to call a lawyer. Not read a book.

They can copy your product, they can't copy your brand

As we discussed in Chapter 3, the key to building a strong brand is having a purpose that goes beyond making a profit – a reason for your brand to exist in the world that isn't rooted in capitalism. This then extends to your values, your tone of voice and your visual identity. It's relatively easy for a competitor to come along and copy your product, choose a similar name and try to adopt the same marketing strategy. But it's much harder for them to copy your purpose and values. Customers can feel this. Copycat brands always lack the depth of the original brand they were 'inspired by', to put it nicely.

Invest in your loyal customers

It's far more time-consuming and expensive to acquire a customer than it is to entice a current customer to repurchase, particularly if your product is a high-quality item that the customer needs to use ongoing. Keep a close eye on your repeat purchase rates and customer reviews – these are metrics, both quantitative and qualitative, that you should deeply care about. After all, it's a two-way street and a good relationship goes both ways. You reward your loyal customers, and they reward you. The easiest way to do this is with a loyalty program. At frank body, this program is called Hotel Pink and we have six figures' worth of members. Each time a member purchases a product, they get points. When they reach a certain number of points they can exchange that for a discount.

Remember

Do not get distracted. Control what you can control and forget the rest.

If you spend your time getting frustrated at copycats, it doesn't do anything to them; it just makes your day worse and distracts you from growing your company.

Give yourself time to be frustrated, but don't obsess over it.

Focus your energy on how to stay ahead. True entrepreneurs and creatives live to create. So use the energy to stay one step ahead of the copycats. Continue to evolve and level up.

THE LESSON:

Show them you're the OG for a reason and you'll not just survive but thrive.

Chapter 11

THE US OF A: CREATING A GLOBAL BRAND

Snow is falling. Christmas decorations are starting to go up. People are dressing up their dogs in tiny snow booties. New York is New York-ing. Bree has bounded downstairs from her hotel room completely enchanted by the romance of snow in the city. In her enthusiasm, she has once again forgotten her gloves. Jess sends her naive best friend back upstairs to get them, knowing in a few minutes Bree's hands will be popsicles and the trip will be ruined.

We're about to walk the few blocks to what will become our first New York office. It's one of those pivotal 'pinch us' moments. Bree comes back downstairs, now more appropriately dressed with gloves, a black train-driver-style hat and big tartan coat. Jess, a winter dressing pro, has gone for her signature fluffy earmuffs, a faux fur coat that Mr Yeti would be proud of and classic leather gloves. Over the last week we've toured offices in LA and New York trying to find 'the one'. And by 'the one' we mean the one our finance team will allow.

We're eight years into business and making our play into the US. This starts with building an on-the-ground team and that means we need somewhere to put them. LA makes more sense with the time difference, the one direct flight and the ethos of the brand. But the talent in New York is much better for our brand, there is more media and, well ... it's New York and it's snowing.

We come to the first WeWork ever built. It's in a classic red brick building in SoHo. It doesn't have the same glossy features some of the new WeWork offices have, and our office here is the size of our storage cupboard in Melbourne. But it's the right size, the right price and it feels right in our gut. We sign the lease, hire the team, and now we have to figure out how to conquer the Big Apple.

For many brands, the US is the ultimate goal. Cracking Australia is great, but the United States has roughly 311 million more people than Australia. The US population is estimated to be around 347 million, while Australia's population is about 27 million.

Financially, that's a lot more lucrative.

From a brand and marketing perspective, the US is a whole new challenge. The biggest challenges with the US are the same as its benefits – size and money.

Those 347 million people are scattered across fifty states. And each state is like its own country. They have their own values, cultural nuances, lexicon and beliefs.

More people means more money, which means more brands with big budgets. If you want to play with the US brands, it's going to cost you. Your dollar does not go as far in the US as it does in Australia.

This is why you need to nail your brand and positioning. Have a well-thought-out plan and the funding to back it.

Over the years, Willow & Blake has worked with many US-based brands and founders.

We helped hair care brand Briogeo (founded by Nancy Twine) to re-establish its brand positioning and tone of voice just before they were acquired by Wella. We completely rebranded The Frontal Queen – a wig company known for their lace wigs – which started in Adey Olaoluwa's garage and now has over 292,000 Instagram followers and is stocked in Urban Outfitters. We also named, designed and built wine brand Good Clean Wine, whose Missouri-based founders let us name their rosé 'Synchronised Swimming'. Legends.

US clients like our irreverent tone of voice, our speed and creativity. It means our team are always thinking globally. We've also helped many Australian brands navigate their international launches, taking learnings from frank body's launch.

Our first trip to the US happened seven months after frank body had launched.

As an ecommerce business, we were global from day one. But the US was the country we had our sights set on. We could see there was already demand. Customers were ordering from our Australian site and paying more than the price of the scrub to ship it to the US.

We decided to find a warehouse and localise shipping. By holding the stock in the US, we freed up enough margin to allow us to offer free, fast shipping.

All five of the founders went on that first trip to meet our new LA-based third-party logistics provider.

3PL, or third-party logistics, refers to the outsourcing of logistics operations – like warehousing, inventory management and order fulfilment – to specialised providers. These providers manage various aspects of the supply chain, allowing businesses to focus on core operations.

We rented a seventies-style house in the Hollywood Hills with a view over the twinkling city reminiscent of a movie set. To complete the movie fantasy, we hired two cars. Steve and Alex got a white Mercedes convertible. Jess, Eri and Bree got a big black Chevrolet, complete with leather interior and tinted windows. Bree was too scared to drive it up the winding hills, so Jess became the designated driver.

Our first mission? Meet our new distribution partner: a lovely man named Dieder who we would end up working with for many, many years.

Dieder took great pride in showing us around the warehouse. It was surreal to see our scrubs sitting there next to all these other well-known brands ready to be shipped out to US customers. Spoiler: when we started offering free, fast shipping our US sales skyrocketed.

Our second mission? Marketing.

We met with our new PR company, brand partners, influencers, media and anyone we thought could help us get the word out there. But before we started pushing heavily into the market, we needed to understand our brand position in the US and how our brand would show up. Would it be different or the same as in Australia? Would we lean into our Australian-made angle? Did the US even care about that?

Over the years, we've done this many times for other brands, and each case needed to be assessed independently.

To start, here's our journey.

frank body's brand already had a clearly defined character – frank. He was your typical Aussie flirt. To try to make him American would be inauthentic.

We leaned into the Australian lifestyle positioning, which aligned with our product and the clear link to skin and the beach. However, we didn't use tired tropes like Crocodile Dundee or only showing blonde beach babes – we showed a modern version of Australia with a diverse array of skin tones.

Our initial strategy was to maintain consistency but localise content for the region.

The brand tone of voice remained largely consistent globally apart from localised spelling and key words (like 'trash' and 'curb'). As we used content creators from all over the world for both lo-fi and campaign imagery, we didn't need to adjust our content hugely, but we did intentionally curate our image selection for the US website to ensure appropriate representation of numerous cultures and skin types.

Once we established a US team we started to create more and more US-specific content. That was their remit, after all. We partnered with very specific influencers, and we created US-specific products like a Cinnabuns Scrub: a sweet cinnamon scrub inspired by the chain Cinnabon. This was backed up with a Snow Scrub that, wildly, was not related to the party drug but instead was white, cool to touch and inspired by the snow Bree had so fondly fawned over earlier.

The content, tone of voice and brand became more and more diluted. We watched on from Australia trying to be open to localised content but eventually made the decision to bring all creative and marketing back to Australia.

Each brand needs to decide its own journey, but it's good to take inspiration from others.

Let's take a look at a few brands who have done it well.

Bluey

To start, we want to look at an out-of-category brand: a cartoon about a little blue heeler. A cartoon all Australian parents would know. A cartoon whose theme song makes you wiggle. A cartoon that is so unapologetically Australian it makes even the most nonchalant of us feel patriotic: *Bluey*.

The children's cartoon is now watched in over sixty countries and in 2025 was the most streamed show of any kind in the US.

What's surprising about the show's US success is how readily the US audience embraced the unique Australian-ness of the characters, plot lines and settings. The Australian accents, the idioms and the subtle cultural nuances Australian audiences love are also loved by the Yanks.

The real success of *Bluey* lies in the storytelling. We always tell our kids we love it because it has lessons in it. And, like many parents, we're often seen with tears streaming down our faces after the storyline hits us in the guts.

For example, the episode called 'Grandad' deals with themes of ageing, loss and the importance of cherishing every moment with your family. These are universal themes that people can relate to regardless of where they are in the world.

The lesson we can all take from *Bluey* is to find the human truth and elements of your brand that translate globally and don't feel you need to whack an American accent on them.

Aesop

Born in Melbourne, Aesop has become a billion-dollar brand largely due to its international success. The brand is known for its discerning, intellectually rigorous tone of voice and exacting minimal branding. The stores are works of art or architectural brilliance and adorned with great philosophers' quotes.

Our favourite copy line is on their Post-Poo Drops:

'In instances where vigorous activity has occurred in the bathroom, dilute several drops of this carefully crafted product in the toilet bowl after flushing, for the benefit of all subsequent visitors.'

Clearly, no Australian accent can be detected in this copy.

Had Aesop decided to lean into their Australian roots, this may have read: 'If someone's gone to town in the dunny, chuck a few drops of this stuff in the bowl.'

Their brand is unique as a luxury Australian brand, and while Melburnians might proudly assert their Australian roots, the overseas market do not know the brand is Australian.

In an interview with the *Australian Financial Review* in 2023, Aesop Chief Customer Officer Suzanne Santos said that the Australian link is very by the by. 'It is a rare admission of nonchalance. I don't think it's a bad thing,' she said of the idea that people don't know Aesop is Australian. 'It doesn't seem to have deterred people from discovering us.'[30]

Suzanne went on to say, 'Dennis (the founder) is never one for a trend. Australiana didn't hold any appeal. We didn't want that inflicted on us.'

The lesson here is that brands do not have to be rooted in a place. Aesop is more akin to a luxury European brand, and its success translates globally.

A chat with Maeva Heim – founder, Bread Beauty Supply

Founded by Australian marketing genius Maeva Heim, Bread Beauty Supply is a hair care brand that aims to change the narrative around textured hair.

Maeva initially pursued a career in marketing for corporate beauty brands like L'Oréal, but felt the industry didn't acknowledge or cater to her hair type. This led her to stop chemically straightening her hair and embrace her natural curls, which highlighted the lack of suitable simple products for textured hair.

Bread Beauty Supply's core mission is to simplify hair care for people with textured hair, offering uncomplicated, practical and fun products.

Maeva wanted the brand's aesthetic and tone to be relatable and fun, with early packaging inspired by her friends and scent profiles reflecting nostalgic, happy memories like Froot Loops cereal milk.

Bread Beauty Supply launched in 2020 straight into Sephora USA online and in store. This is no small feat for a brand founded in Perth, Australia.

In 2025, the company was acquired by Cost of Doing Business – a holding company founded by Olamide Olowe, the founder of trailblazing body care brand Topicals.

Maeva is proud of her Australian roots and publicly speaks to her founder story, growing up in Perth and working in her mum's salon.

But for her, the opportunity in the US was too big to ignore.

For many Australian brands, cracking the US comes after proof of concept in Australia. However, Maeva flipped this trajectory – so we asked her how and why.

You launched in the US before launching in Australia. Did you always know the US customer was your target?

I knew before we launched that the US would be our primary market, for a few reasons. The first was that my ambition was to create a global brand that could come out swinging. I knew that would require scale and venture funding. Since I knew what the end goal was, I was able to work backwards from there, and understand that to get venture funding as an early-stage brand, I would need it to be a US company that operates in the US first and foremost. This would allow venture capitalists to say 'yes' with much less complexity. They wouldn't have to worry about the tax implications of investing in an Australian company, or have doubts about our ability to crack the US audience later down the track.

How did you secure your placement in Sephora pre-launch?

It's a bit of a longwinded story, but the first thing I did was set a goal. The goal was to secure ranging in Sephora USA before we had produced a single product. I knew that as an early-stage brand, I would need some wins on the board in order to secure capital before we started selling and before we could show revenue. Sephora was a natural goal given the growth they were seeing in their hair category, and the lack of options they had for curly and coily hair types at the time. I approached a Sephora USA buyer at an event and pitched my idea right there on the spot. That conversation led to an email, which led to a meeting, and many months later a contract that would see us launching on sephora.com and into 150 Sephora USA stores before we had even launched.

Are there any differences in the way the brand shows up in Australia versus the US?

Definitely! I think the Australian customer, by nature of the Australian culture, is much more sarcastic, and a little less conservative than the average customer in the US. Jokes and certain sayings don't always translate, so it's something to be really conscious of. I do have a thesis that it's easier to translate a US brand to an Australian one than it is the other way around. So, if you're launching a brand that you intend to launch into the US later on, make sure you're taking this into account when thinking about your brand tone.

Are there any key differences in the way you market in the US versus Australia?

I was super intentional about creating a brand that could be international from day one. So although we started in the US, when we looked at our early customer archetypes, we were really conscious of the 'Bread girl' being an international customer. I would say that because of that, there are huge differences in the way we market the brand in the US versus Australia. We tend to start with the US first, and then translate those ideas and marketing messages into the Australian market. We take note of language differences, but the actual tactics tend to remain pretty consistent. One of the major differences, though, is community. We have a much stronger emphasis on community-driven campaigns in the US. Because the market is so much more mature, having a healthy mix of community marketing and ambassadorships is extremely important, whereas it's not as much of a focus for us in the Australian market because the infrastructure around community building is so different (read: behind).

What is your advice for other Australian entrepreneurs looking to crack the US market?

I would say to have a very, very good understanding of the white space you're trying to occupy. You need to become a student of the market. Understand all the retail players and the brands that occupy them within your category. Build a solid thesis around what's missing (this can be a combination of your product proposition, brand proposition, distribution angle, etc.) and how you plan to effectively fill that space. Listen to your current customers and what they love about your brand, and then research how that could translate to the US market to fill a space. The industry is crowded, yes, but there is always room for true differentiation and your interpretation of what can and should exist.

Key Advice for Writing or Creating a Brand for the US Market

Understand regional diversity

The US is not a monolith – consumer preferences differ across states, cities and cultural groups. Research regional markets (e.g. Midwest, West Coast and South) and tailor your approach accordingly. Don't fall into clichés or tired tropes. Get to understand the specific cultural references that your audience do, otherwise you'll look like a tourist trying to fit in.

Use American English

Adapt spelling (e.g. color/colour), idioms and tone to reflect American communication norms. Avoid overly formal or British expressions unless they align with your brand's identity. Check that common words translate well locally. See a list below of words that differ between the US and Australia.

Australia	**United States**
Rubbish	Trash/garbage
Bin	Trash can/garbage can
Petrol	Gas/gasoline
Ute	Pickup truck
Thongs	Flip-flops
Boot (of a car)	Trunk
Bonnet (of a car)	Hood
Lollies	Candy
Biscuit	Cookie
Chips (hot)	Fries

Chips (packet)	Potato chips
Capsicum	Bell pepper
Coriander	Cilantro
Prawn	Shrimp
Singlet	Tank top
Jumper	Sweater
Footpath	Sidewalk
Torch	Flashlight
Nappy	Diaper
Dummy (baby)	Pacifier
Chemist	Pharmacy/drugstore
Car park	Parking lot
Holiday	Vacation
Letterbox	Mailbox
Mobile (phone)	Cell (phone)
Postcode	Zip code
Sultanas	Raisins
Esky	Cooler/Ice chest
Servo	Gas station
Bottle-o	Liquor store
Brekkie	Breakfast
Loo	Bathroom/restroom
Fairy floss	Cotton candy

Comply with US regulations

Make sure your product labelling, advertising and business practices meet US federal and state regulations (e.g. FDA, FTC and state laws). This is particularly important for packaging that is not easily updated. Compliance regulations differ from country to country, so get a local advisor to review your claims and copy to ensure your compliance. No one likes getting a letter from a US lawyer that your customers are forming a class action lawsuit against you.

Decide your stance on holidays and cultural events

If you try to celebrate every holiday, you'll go crazy. Pick the key ones that mean something to your brand and your customers. Maybe that's NY Pride March in June or National Sunscreen Day (27 May).

Some holidays are celebrated on the same day (Mother's Day), but others are different (Father's Day).

A chat with Shaun Wilson – co-founder, Bondi Sands

Bondi Sands, the iconic Australian self-tanning brand, was founded in 2012 by Blair James and Shaun Wilson with a simple but powerful idea: bring salon-quality tanning into the homes of everyday Australians.

Inspired by Bondi Beach and its sun-soaked lifestyle, the brand set out to bottle the feeling of an 'Australian tan'. From humble beginnings in local pharmacies, Bondi Sands quickly expanded into global markets including New Zealand, the UK and the US. The brand has worked with some of the world's biggest celebrities, including Kylie Jenner and Paris Hilton.

Eventually the brand caught the eye of global beauty giant Kao Corporation, which acquired the brand in 2023 for nearly $450 million.

The CEO of Bondi Sands, Shaun, is one of the hardest working, smartest and loveliest founders we've had the pleasure of knowing and working with. There was no shortage of topics we could have explored with Shaun but for this conversation, we focused on two key themes: international growth and leadership.

What was the moment you realised Bondi Sands was going to be bigger than just Australia? Was global always your strategy?

Global was always our strategy. In the first year, Blair and I wrote down what the brand should stand for. We asked: how can we ensure our brand travels? How the brand could go beyond Australia was part of every decision.

In terms of when we *knew* we had an international brand; that came in 2015. We had strong success in Australia quite quickly and then we launched in the UK. We believed the Bondi lifestyle, the Australian personality and the imagery we were utilising in our marketing could capture the UK audience. And we were right. They got it. Boots and Superdrug, the two big retailers, understood it quickly and we had a lot of success there.

Why did you choose the UK over the US?

From a brand point of view, we believed the story would resonate quicker with UK consumers. Also, in terms of resources and our business model, it was more fiscally responsible to go to the UK first. I don't think there's a right or wrong, but I do believe the US is the most challenging market simply because of how big it is. You need to pick the right states, the right retailers, the right partners, build the right team. You don't want to get that wrong.

And in the UK, how did you how did you structure your entry into that market? Did you use a distributor?

We met our UK distributor at CosmoProf in America, would you believe? We were trying to get more exposure through trade shows, and I met Stephen Short from Intermark. He got the brand straight away.

But what I believe – and I've always been strong on this – is that even if you appoint a distributor in a key market, you can't outsource everything. I'm really against that. We structured it as a joint team and that benefited both the retailer and the end customer.

That's been our strategic model in every big market – Germany, Canada, the US. And over time, we've built our own full teams and phased out the distributor model. But in the beginning, a brand lead with the distributor was the right model to ensure growth and maintain brand control.

What market did you go into after the UK?

We went into several European markets (Scandinavia, Germany, Ireland), all of which were really successful for us. Then we expanded into Canada, which was another big market. Again, we used the same model: a brand lead working alongside a distributor. Strategically, we had always wanted to enter the US, and by that stage we were the number one self-tanning brand in Australia, New Zealand, the UK, parts of Europe, and Canada. We felt ready to enter the US in 2019, but the planning started back in late 2017.

You've spoken a bit about how Bondi Sands was positioning itself as an Australian brand. Did you lean

into that when you went into international markets like the UK and the US or did you localise for the American market?

I'm big on 'Think global, act local'. Thinking global means the brand values, the brand principles and pillars must be adhered to – that's non-negotiable. What you do localise are the tweaks in terms of comms. What are the key call-outs that make more sense for the customer mix in that market? From a cultural point of view, from a storytelling point of view, and from a performance point of view?

For example, 'Number one' in the UK probably has stronger merit than it does in Australia, in certain areas of the planogram. So you've got to work with the right marketing leads to understand that. Not just a nationwide call-out – even a retailer-specific call-out is really important.

What advice do you have for other founders or entrepreneurs who are currently just servicing the Australian market but looking to expand overseas? Are there any key indicators they can look for to know when the time is right to expand into international markets?

Honestly, it's hard to answer that question for every brand because they're all so different. Finances are an important place to start. Do you have the right revenue metric within your home country? Are you comfortable enough to expand overseas? What resources are you going to put towards that? Do you believe it's the right decision to ensure future growth?

You need to look at your brand holistically. You can't just look at one area. Make the decision that's right for the *whole* brand.

To me, the brand isn't just your visual identity or your marketing strategy – it's everything you do: customer service, supply chain, delivery. That's all part of the brand. And I think good leaders are really the CEOs of every department. So, a founder needs to take that full view when making the decision to expand. Is this really going to improve every part of my brand? Will it strengthen the whole ecosystem? If so, then it might be the right time to go.

Let's talk about the US for a minute. A very common question is 'How do you crack the US?' We've seen some Australian brands struggle but Bondi Sands succeeded. Were there any key tactics that helped you win in that market?

Definitely. I think you need to treat the US like a roadmap and understand what the first few hurdles are. From a marketing standpoint, we believed in being disruptive. So even before we entered the US, we asked, 'How can we build brand awareness first?' It's a big investment, and you don't get a return straight away. But how can we make noise? We decided the first step was getting a big influencer to talk about our brand. We engaged Kylie Jenner.

At the time, we were only selling through ecommerce. We didn't have any retail presence. But she did some amazing content for us, and it went viral globally. That was massive. It helped people take notice of us and of the category.

And what about your bricks-and-mortar strategy?

My advice to founders is always: look at a retailer not just through *your* lens as a brand, but through *theirs*. What are *they* trying to achieve? Are they targeting gen Z? Are they focused on skin health? Are they lacking innovation? Do they want disruption? I used to read annual reports to understand what a retailer was doing before I'd even meet with them. That way, I'd walk into a meeting already understanding their strategy. I could then ask: How can our brand help them serve their current customers and attract new ones?

We went into Walgreens very prepared. They gave us more than we ever expected: a national rollout across 10,000 stores, strong in-store presence, real focus. And I believe that came from understanding their strategy, offering them something valuable, and aligning our marketing teams to make a real impact in the category.

Did you spend time in the US? Did you or Blair ever move there?

Yes – and that's a really important point. Between Blair and I, we probably spent at least six years overseas, cumulatively, out of the last eleven. A lot of that was in the UK and US, being on the ground with our teams, retailers and customers. Being present while building the team. I'd love to say you can do it all from Melbourne, but the reality is that if you want alignment and culture, you need to travel.

What was the biggest personal sacrifice that came with scaling a global business?

As a CEO and leader, you spend a lot of time alone. That's one thing people might not realise. And I don't mean alone in a physical sense – it's more of a mental thing. You're with your thoughts a lot.

When you put a lot of pressure on yourself or the brand to perform, you mentally carry that pressure. You're thinking things through all the time, and you're alone in those thoughts. So it's about pushing through that. Other than that, I don't really see any sacrifices. I just loved every moment.

THE LESSON:

Learn from those who have been there and done that.

Chapter 12

WHEN MECCA CALLS

We walk into a room filled with hundreds of MECCA staff. They are standing, cheering and waving star-shaped plastic clapping devices with an enthusiasm normally reserved for mad sports enthusiasts or pop stars. The stage is filled with a plush aubergine couch, a red chair for each founder and an array of colour-adjacent flowers sits perfectly positioned between the custom wall decal and the soft furnishings. It's like walking into a giant MECCA gift bag – a blur of pinks, purples and reds. It smells great. And it almost feels too fancy to touch. On stage is Marita Burke, the Chief MECCA-Maginations Officer. Her hair is perfectly blow-waved, her lipstick matches the aubergine couch and her warm voice cuts through the clapping. 'We are so excited to welcome the frank body founders to the MECCA family,' she begins, but again is quickly drowned out by the sound of hundreds of women and a few men screaming and waving their plastic clapping stars. By this stage we're all quietly questioning if this is a cult – but to be honest, even if it was, we'd all be guzzling the Kool-Aid.

Founded in 1997 by the force of nature Jo Horgan, MECCA started with a single Melbourne store on Toorak Road. This was a store we had visited many times, starting with our addiction to NARS Laguna bronzer in our early twenties, extending to our love affair with bareMinerals Complexion Rescue in our late twenties and continuing into our Charlotte Tilbury era in our thirties.

Today, MECCA boasts over one hundred stores across Australia and New Zealand and is reported to be a billion-dollar business, making it one of the most influential beauty retailers globally.

Rewind twelve months to when they popped up in our inbox.

That's right. MECCA came to us.

Bricks-and-mortar retail expansion had not been part of our business plan. For us, the beauty of having our own brand was having full creative control over every single detail. And a straight ecommerce play allowed us to do that.

Digital retail was a cost-effective way to create and maintain the impression we wanted the customer to have. Physical retail would be a big and expensive adjustment.

Through digital, we could control how consumers found us, and then drive their purchase journey from when they landed on the website to how the product arrived. We could ensure every element was customised – every email, every text, every interaction. We trained our staff not only to know the products back to front but to know the brand and tone of voice

Physical retail does not allow for that level of control. The thought of a coffee scrub sitting alone on a shelf waiting for a sales assistant to explain its benefits made us feel uneasy.

There was also the small issue that we had not factored retail margins, retail marketing or capital expenditure into our pricing strategy.

It's comparatively easy to manage your profit and loss through one ecommerce channel. You know how much you're spending and how much you're selling. The data is clean, so you can start to predict your repeat purchases and accurately forecast your ordering.

At frank, we quickly learned the difference between sell-in and sell-out. We made a conscious decision as a business to always focus on sell-out (the time at which a customer buys it off the shelf, rather than when the retailer buys it from you, the brand).

We will never forget the response we had from Alyce Tran when we congratulated her for getting her brand The Daily Edited into a key US retailer. She said, 'Don't congratulate me now, congratulate me if we're still there in three years' time. Getting into a retailer is easy – you're selling to one or two category managers. Sell-out is the challenge.'

We never forgot that lesson.

Retail was a whole new ball game. The risk was high, but so was the reward. And MECCA is the Super Bowl. Most beauty brand founders would wet themselves at the opportunity to have their brand stocked in MECCA. The fact that they came to us was a big deal.

Steve, our co-founder and CEO at frank body, was very bullish on retail. He saw the potential where others (Bree) saw risk. The decision to go into retail was one we debated rigorously.

At the time, the business was in a state of flux. More and more brands were flooding onto Instagram. Influencer marketing had tripled in cost. Our organic growth had slowed. We'd already invested in a large team to support our phenomenal original growth and now needed to find new ways to maintain the growth we had become accustomed to. Retail offered us a whole new revenue channel.

Call it naivety, but our lack of experience in the beauty industry worked in our favour. Much to MECCA's surprise, we didn't jump. In fact, we came back very cautiously and entered into a robust negotiation. It was a meeting with MECCA founder Jo Horgan herself that calmed our nerves and gained them our trust.

Then the fun started. Led by Steve, we signed a deal with MECCA and got to work on how the brand would show up in a retail environment.

Placement

Most retail stores have specific categories, and placement for your brand or product is predetermined. For example, all of the skincare brands are in the skincare section; all the hair care brands are in the hair care section.

One of our goals with frank body was to bring the energy and sexiness of colour cosmetics to the skincare category. Therefore, we didn't want to be where the other skincare brands were. We wanted to be with the colour cosmetics, with our own gondola.

At the time, this wasn't done. Skin care was housed on shelves at the back and sides of the stores and makeup was housed in gondolas in the centre. The reason for this is shelf productivity – a two-centimetre lipstick sells for $80, whereas a coffee scrub is 10 centimetres wide and sells for $16. To make these numbers work, we needed volume. But again, frank isn't your normal skincare brand – and MECCA isn't your usual retailer.

We worked together to create an incredible brand experience that reflected how we showed up online, with a little more elevation. The results? Huge productivity. Having our own gondola allowed us to tell the frank body story and educate on the shelf. We ensured we had pictures of the product in use and made space for brand copy like our original tagline – 'Get naked, get dirty, get rough, get clean'. MECCA understood that our brand pushed boundaries and their customers loved it.

TIP: Think about out-of-category placement and how you can meet your customer where they are shopping.

Packaging

At Willow & Blake we've worked with brands in all categories, from fast-moving consumer goods (FMCG), pharmacy and grocery to specialty retail and owned stores. Whatever the placement we know the key to making the space work hard is the right packaging. Packaging should reflect your brand and your key messages and, most importantly, be functional. Boxes that don't stand up by themselves is not the first impression you want to make.

At frank body, our original ecommerce packaging did not include boxes. We wanted to elevate the brand experience for the retail environment, so we considered the boxes to be an additional space for marketing. They allowed more real estate for copy and again allowed us to communicate more of what made the brand unique.

TIP: Retail and ecommerce packaging serve different purposes.

Launch

'One million babes already love me. Let me charm you in person for the first time ever.'

That was the copy line emblazoned across every MECCA Maxima (since renamed to MECCA) store in Australia. We went big for the launch, with a full national window takeover, off-location coffee pop-ups in store, a staff education roadshow, press tour and influencer events.

Launching with MECCA changed the trajectory of the business. In the eyes of consumers, we were now a legitimate business – not just 'that Instagram brand'.

For us as founders, it gave us a much-needed confidence boost. Trying to explain to our parents and people outside the industry that we sold purely online and mainly through Instagram was often met with a raised eyebrow and 'Don't quit your day job' or a patronising 'How's your little side hustle going?'

Over the next eleven years, we would launch into over 7000 stores around the world. This included Urban Outfitters, Ulta and Walmart in the US; Liberty, Selfridges and Boots in the UK; and Sephora in Europe, South-East Asia and Canada. We also started wholesale distribution in the Nordics and Middle East. To complement our Australian retail offering, we launched our sub-brand Everyday by frank body into Priceline and Coles.

Each retailer gave us a new set of challenges and learnings, but also a new set of customers and opportunities.

TIP: You only get one chance to make a good first impression. Launch with a bang.

Steve Rowley – co-founder and CEO, frank body

On expanding into wholesale and retail

For the last twelve years, Steve has been frank body's CEO. He developed the original recipe for the coffee scrub, and has done everything from to negotiating million-dollar deals to staying on to steer the ship when the three other co-founders stepped down. Steve's role in frank's journey is not as well documented as other founders', as he prefers to remain something of an enigma, but clearly frank would not exist without him.

As his wife, Bree has had the pleasure of witnessing this man in many roles since they met at the tender ages of twenty-two and twenty-five. They met the old-fashioned way; at a bar. Jess was there watching.

After bailing out of a horticulture degree one semester in, Steve did what he was always supposed to do – work for himself. Alongside frank body, he has built and sold over fourteen businesses. He is a force of nature, and when he sets his mind to doing something, it gets done.

While Steve's role is far more encompassing than just retail, he set his sights on growth, leading the retail expansion of frank body into over 2000 bricks-and-mortar stores worldwide. As an expert in this field, we asked him for his advice on how to navigate the wonderful world of retail. What follows are Steve's own words.

Rule #1. Sell-out over sell-in: shelf fill doesn't pay the bills

Rule #1 at frank body has always been that a product is not really sold until it's in the shower. What does that mean? Sell-out (which means your product has been sold to the consumer by the retailer) performance is always far more important that sell-in performance. 'Sell-in' means the product you sell to a retailer – it can mean sales like shelf fill (the product retailers buy to fill their shelves) or replenishment orders. Million-dollar shelf fill orders (sell-in) can be great for the business ego and finance department, but they mean little unless the customer and end users are picking them up off the shelf and taking them home (sell-out).

Rule #2. Retail = detail: understand retail contribution margin

The devil is in the detail, so understanding the contract and how a retailer monetises their platform (aka hidden costs) is key. Over the years, our frank body team has become more and more focused on channel contribution margin. This way of looking at a sales channel means we understand completely what it costs to do business with a particular retailer. 'Contribution margin' looks at sales (sell-in), gross margin (sales – product costs and associated freight), direct marketing (retailer charges for their marketing), chargebacks (retailer charges for late delivery fees, or destroying unsaleable stock) and direct staffing costs (the allowance for our staffing costs directly relating to running the account). It was not uncommon to find that some of our most important accounts had months and even years being contribution margin negative.

Rule #3. Get on her shopping list: don't count on the sales assistant

Performing well in retail is all about driving foot traffic in store (even better if you can drive foot traffic *to* store) to pick up your product off the shelf. Once the customer is there, it's about standing out on the shelf while clearly showcasing your value proposition to the customer. This is crucial in a crowed shelf environment. We always talked about how we are getting on the shopping list, what our marketing team are doing to make frank body top of mind as our potential customer strolls the store aisles. We were never dependent on the sales assistant doing the work for us.

Rule #4. Get out of category: checkouts, endcaps and minis are small spots with big impact

Shelf space is your retail home, but nothing beats out-of-category opportunities. Examples of these are the product spots near checkouts, at the end of product aisles, travel minis, gifting shelving and other types of spaces away from your standard product shelf, which is typically in a fixed location. These opportunities (that can be awarded, earned or bought) provide excellent possibilities to get more eyes on your brand, helping with the all-important awareness task of brand marketing.

Rule #5. Treat your buyer like a business partner: when they win, you win

Your buyer's goals and targets are your goals and targets. When they win, you win. Retail buyers are notoriously time-poor, passionate about the beauty industry and will also hold the keys to the opportunities you get to see. For frank body, we have always been very cognisant of how we manage this relationship, how we can make the buyer's job easier and ensure we work within an established key set of structures that allows us both to work efficiently and effectively. Simple things like sending pre-read presentations prior to a meeting, running on time, knowing your data and even taking printouts of your presentation in case of technical issues. The more seriously you take this relationship, the more reliable you act as a partner, the more you will ensure you continue to hold the partnership in good stead.

Rule #6. Sales and marketing must work together: one team, one dream

Sales and marketing work hand in hand – this is probably the most crucial of all my key tips, as it underpins them all. When your brand is strong and your marketing is effective, the consumer demand created will assist in solving a significant number of issues. This relates back to all the points above: store footfall, product awareness and consideration, getting on the shopping list, buyer relationships and good effective marketing will apply grease to these crucially important cogs.

THE LESSON:

When one door closes, pry open a window.

Chapter 13

CULTURE AND HOW TO BUILD IT

'When work doesn't feel like work, you know the culture is good.'
– a real quote from a Willow & Blake employee

Culture is one of those things that everyone talks about, but few actually understand.

Culture isn't Friday night drinks, a ping pong table and some motivational posters on the wall.

It's how a team functions, why you come to work every day and how you feel when you're there.

It starts at the top, but culture is created by every person in the organisation. It's driven by the leaders, but it's lived by the collective.

Culture can make or break a business.

In just two years, we went from a team of four to twenty-five. We became our own bosses at the ages of twenty-three and twenty-four respectively. This meant we didn't get to have a lot of managers ourselves and we had precisely no on-the-job training outside of our own businesses.

We learned through a baptism of fire that being the boss of a startup means you're not just the boss. You're also a counsellor, the office manager, logistics coordinator, tax advice consultant, IT support, nutritionist, hobby coordinator and the team's mum. When there's a problem, you are the adult who needs to solve it – even if you don't know how or it has nothing to do with your actual business. Bad breakup? You're up. And that is a lot of pressure to handle when you're also trying to figure out how to run a business.

We made a lot of mistakes in the early days, but for the most part the culture at frank body and Willow & Blake has been incredible and the thing we are most proud of. Leadership training was something we both invested in and continue to invest in – anyone who manages a team should. But largely, we figured out how to lead through our own research and trial and error. Over fifteen years, we've learned a few things.

Building a Great Team

'The team that gets you from zero to one million isn't the same team that gets you from one to ten million, which isn't the same team that gets you from ten million to one hundred million.'

Dan Monheit, one of Bree's mentors, gave her this piece of advice while they were walking the streets of Prahran. It became a key learning for us at frank body as we scaled and evolved our team. Sometimes a team member grows with a brand, but sometimes a brand outgrows a team member. Everyone has their own next chapter, even founders.

We have hired so many brilliant people over the years, and we feel very lucky to have worked alongside them. But of course, there were some learning curves along the way. Interviewing well is a skill we wish we had honed earlier. Our top piece of advice to everyone who runs interviews is to stop asking leading questions. You will never get to know the candidate properly if you tell them what you want to hear. The second most important lesson is that impatience will kill your business. Don't settle for the person in front of you right now – instead, settle for nothing other than the right person.

Often, we spend more time with the people we work with than we do our friends or family. Building a team that is supportive, ambitious and that makes us excited to go to work has been one of the greatest privileges of the frank and Willow & Blake journeys.

Step 1: Hire well

How and who you hire will be different at different stages of your business journey, but one tip that applies to all stages is to hire for values and potential, not just skills. Piecing together a team means knowing your values and hiring people who align with them.

The early stages

In the early stages, we hired what we could afford and who we could find. That means friends, friends of friends and people around our ages or younger. At ages twenty-four and twenty-five, that meant our team were basically infants.

We were like family. We were at a stage of life where work was our life. We worked together, worked out together and partied together. It was fun. However, it also led to many issues around accountability and double-handling. We created makeshift systems, but we were still on the tools and micromanaging most of it.

TIP FOR THIS STAGE: Don't hire mini-yous – as tempting as it might be. Hire for your gaps and the tasks you don't enjoy.

The middle stages

In the middle stages, we had more budget and more wisdom. We hired specialists in their roles. We found talent that had skills we didn't. We started to learn to let go and delegate. This was messy at first, but it was important. We struggled to let go and put in the right hierarchy.

TIP FOR THIS STAGE: Hire people smarter than you and let go of your ego. Remember that you got to where you are by doing things differently. Don't try to start acting like a big corporation.

The established stage

As our businesses became established, we hired a senior Heads of Department team and they hired the people below them. We focused on keeping great people, offering share schemes and long-term incentives. We moved from star players to coaching roles. This is apparently the sweet spot, but funnily enough, once you get here you start to miss the old days when your life wasn't back-to-back meetings.

TIP FOR THIS STAGE: Don't do meetings for the sake of meetings; remember that you create the life you lead and you're the boss. If something isn't aligned to your values, change the structure or your role.

Step 2: Onboard and train well

One of the most common challenges we hear founders face is letting go of control. The image that comes into our heads when we think of this is of a child nodding that they will let go while creating a vice-like grip on whatever they are holding. Bree cringes when she thinks of the micromanagement style she had for the first years of both her businesses. If you worked for her then – apologies. She was also learning.

The beauty and curse of founder life is that you learn to do everything, so you will always be comparing the way something is done to how you used to do it. In some cases, this is good. Mostly, it's bad. For us to grow, we had to learn to relinquish control and upskill others. This started with customer service and social media. For weeks, Bree disapproved up to 50 per cent of the content our team created. But instead of giving useful feedback, she would change or redo the work. All this did was piss her off, because she was overworked. It pissed the team off because they felt undervalued and no one learned or progressed. Eventually, Bree realised this was hindering progress and she stopped fixing and resenting. Instead, she started teaching, explaining and (most importantly) listening.

To go from a star player to coach you have to learn to explain why you do things a certain way. Trying to explain our gut instincts and strategy meant going deeper on what we wanted frank and Willow & Blake to be as brands. A key part of this was creating great onboarding documents and ways of working or processes.

As Jess writes this, she has to confess an honest truth: at this point in her career, she doesn't like managing people. Don't let that be confused with not liking them. Working with people is brilliant, but managing them and managing them well is a whole other kettle of fish and a full-time job in itself. It's hilarious to Jess how little managing some managers actually do. She knew she wanted more flexibility, autonomy and to not have recurring meetings in her calendar after fifteen years of being a slave to her diary. This meant she simply couldn't have direct reports, and stepping away from people management was absolutely the right decision for her and the team.

It's crucial to be honest with yourself as you grow into your business about whether you are the right person to do the people management. If you're not, step aside and let someone who loves it do it. You'll be happier and so will your people. That doesn't mean Jess is absent – she does a lot of congratulating and providing feedback behind the scenes with our employees on an ad hoc basis to ensure we stay connected.

A key part of our onboarding is our guiding principles.

We had a beautiful team member at frank body, Pete McKinsey. He was tall, kind and gave us many gifts over the years, both in the form of nuggets of wisdom and nuggets of chocolate from his next role. But the greatest gift he gave was when he told us to write down our guiding principles. We went away to a beach house along the Great Ocean Road armed with butcher's paper, Post-it notes and product samples.

With the waves lapping in the background, we came up with two great things that day.

First was the shimmer scrub: a product that would go on to have a waitlist of tens of thousands of people, sell out multiple times and generate a new wave of hype for the brand.

The other outcome was our guiding principles.

The scrub made us lots of money. The guiding principles gave us and our team direction. Guiding principles shape how you and your team interact on a day-to-day basis. They might not be important when it's just you and your co-founder, but as your brand gets bigger and you start to onboard new team members, they become a valuable asset to ensure the culture you want lives on.

How are they different from brand values?

Brand values are tied to the brand identity and how the company interacts with its customers. They represent the core beliefs that a brand stands for. Unlike guiding principles, brand values can be adjusted or expanded to reflect changes in the market, societal norms or the evolving identity of the brand.

Guiding principles are the fundamental philosophies that shape how a company operates. They relate specifically to the team and people working with the business. They serve as a moral compass, guiding decision-making, actions and behaviours. Guiding principles are deeply ingrained in the company's culture and are typically not altered.

There can be overlap between the two.

Here are ours for frank body:

- Risk it for the biscuit
- Own your actions
- Get shit done
- Differences make us who we are

And for Willow & Blake:

- Be patient and persistent
- Be kind and curious
- Sometimes a blue curtain is just a blue curtain
- Differences make us who we are

We take every employee through these when they start, but that's not enough. You must live your guiding principles. As a leader, you have to model the behaviour you want to see. If you want a team that's creative, collaborative and accountable, then you need to show up that way consistently. People don't follow policies, they follow people. Refer back to your principles constantly – in meetings, in reviews, in every decision you make. The more you repeat them and live them, the more your team will remember them. Eventually they become integrated into the culture.

An example onboarding deck:

- The story so far, because to build the future you need to understand the past
- Our purpose
- Our mission
- Our brand values
- Our product philosophy
- Our customers

- A snapshot of each department
- The people you will be working with
- The culture incentives
- A checklist of tasks to complete

Setting your new hire up for success also means ensuring they have a clear job description, KPIs and a progression plan from day one. For senior team members, we also add self-created and managed 30-, 60- and 90-day plans as one of their first tasks.

Clarity is key. You don't need complicated HR systems; you need simple frameworks that everyone can follow.

Step 3: Stay human and stay connected

Over the years, Bree has gone through phases of intentional disconnection from the team. At one stage, the team was her family. She said hello to everyone in the office every morning. We hugged each other goodbye after meetings. The whole office came to her wedding. As we got bigger, Bree felt she needed to put distance between herself and the team. She stopped having lunch with them. She stopped going to drinks on Friday. She felt a need to make it clear that she was the boss and there was a hierarchy. She stopped crying in goodbye speeches – in fact, she stopped showing much emotion at work at all. She tried to be a calm leader, in control at all times. She tried to emulate the leadership style she admired in others – sure, confident and powerful. But it wasn't her.

Bree is an emotional person. She's a person who craves connection. One day, she started to lean into her strengths and lead with vulnerability. If she didn't know the answer to something, she would say that she needed more information before she could make a decision. If she made a mistake, she owned it. She sat with the team at lunch. She started to share more about who she was as a person, not just a leader. And she started to check in, not just check up on the team. She became clear with her expectations and held herself and the team accountable. She made tough but fair decisions and always explained her rationale. And by doing so, we created a culture that was safe; a team that could speak up, make mistakes and ask questions without fear. It didn't mean becoming everyone's best friend. It meant becoming a leader who was connected and respected.

Jess went through an almost identical journey, intentionally creating space between herself and the team to allow herself to be able to lead with clarity and kindness. Deep friendships were still formed, but in the later years the basis of them was different and more authentic to the ones formed in frank body's early years. The focus of Jess's leadership style is the ethos that 'clarity is kindness'. She sees it as her job to make quick and clear decisions, to set the tone and provide concise, actionable feedback for the team so that they can do their best work and feel confident in what they are working towards. There is no room for murkiness or indecision. One of the greatest compliments of Jess's career was from her second-in-command, Ali, who upon moving on from the company after an amazing tenure thanked her for their time together, telling her she should be proud for leading the department with kindness, clarity and creating such a psychologically safe workspace. Jess had never thought much about the concept of psychological safety at work, but was grateful that Ali defined it this way. Jess had taken over a decade to craft her leadership style. That's a lot of hours, soul searching, reading, coaching and failures to get to this point. Among all the highs and lows of her career, this simple moment is one of the best memories Jess has.

Key takeaways

- You don't have to perform leadership. People don't need you to be perfect. They need you to be present, honest and human.

- Connection builds trust – and trust builds culture. A strong culture starts with leaders who show up as themselves. Share who you are, not just what you do.
- Check in, don't just check up. Ask how your team is *feeling*, not just how they're *performing*. Remember that we're all humans at the end of the day.

Step 4: Fire well

Letting someone go is the worst part of being a leader, but not letting the wrong person go is worse. It affects morale, energy and performance. We've kept people too long before, out of guilt, fear and friendship. But when you delay a hard decision, it only gets worse.

When we had to make these decisions in the early days, it would tear Bree up. She would delay it as long as possible. And when the inevitable meeting would come, her body would be in fight-or-flight mode. Her mouth would go dry. She'd read the prepared script that she took from the internet like a robot, afraid to say anything that could be wrong. There was nothing human about it. It's still the worst part of the job, but over the years we've found ways to make it easier.

Here are some ways to make a goodbye easier.

Be clear, be kind and don't avoid what needs to be done

If someone isn't the right fit for a role or a company, they probably feel it too. Firstly, you need to create a culture of open feedback that is delivered quickly. Don't wait for quarterly reviews – that's not fair to the employee, the team or yourself. Give feedback regularly. Nothing should be a surprise in reviews.

Use a good HR consultant

Firstly, a good HR consultant will help ensure you follow the law. They can also help you draft a script that feels human. Secondly, they can support the team member both during the meeting and after. We always like to offer a free resume health check and career counselling to assist them in finding a job that's a better fit.

References and referrals

Just because the employee wasn't the right fit for you doesn't mean they shouldn't get a reference. Help them to find a new role that's better suited with an honest reference that highlights their strengths.

Communicate

People talk. It's important to get ahead of the gossip. Tell the team as soon as possible, but keep it respectful. You shouldn't share the details. Focus on the facts and the future. Be open to questions, but remember there's a time and place for each conversation.

THE LESSON:

Hire well and fire well.

Chapter 14

EVOLVE OR DIE

When she was thirteen, Jess cut her hair into a jaw-scraping bob with a fringe. She blow-waved that fringe like a tiny veranda for her face every single day and tucked the bottom of her hair so it curled in towards her face. It was like a little frizzy brown helmet (not too different from Lord Farquaad's hair in *Shrek*), offset by braces with multicoloured bands as she commenced the delightful teen experience of straightening her teeth. It worked in 1999, but imagine if she never changed her hair again. Set-and-forget isn't a good policy for life – not for how we do our hair, and certainly not for business strategy.

There's a saying, 'If you're not embarrassed by the first prototype of your brand, you launched too late'. This feels very true for us.

If we look back at where Willow & Blake and frank body were when we first launched, we can see that our brands look very different today. They sound a bit different, too. However, our purpose and our values have always stayed consistent. And this, we believe, is the key to a strong brand evolution. Change to stay relevant to your audience and environment, but don't lose sight of who you are and what you stand for.

frank body's original visual identity can be summed up in one word: simple. Which, to be fair, was the whole point. We had one product, one message and a simple visual identity made up of three colours and one typeface. The packaging was a plain brown coffee bag with a sticker that wrapped over the top. The only elements on the front of the pack were the words '220g of tough love' accompanied by our logo.

As an ecommerce brand, we educated customers through our website. This was also very simple. The first thing you saw when you landed on the home page was a picture of the Original Coffee Scrub and a 'shop now' button. If you scrolled down, there was a small section that listed the ingredients and 'how to use' instructions. No campaign imagery. No animation. Just a white-edged image of the scrub and a questionable illustration of a shower head and a tap.

Was it a master lesson in design? No. Did it convert? Heck, yes.

It was perfect for when we launched, but as all good brands do, it had to evolve to meet the changing needs of the business, the values of the consumer and the expectations of the cultural zeitgeist.

At both Willow & Blake and frank body we continually ask ourselves and our clients one simple question: does our current brand represent who we are and what we do?

If the answer is no, it's time for change.

According to Charles Darwin's *On the Origin of Species*, it is not the most intellectual species that survives, nor the strongest. It's the species that is best able to adapt and adjust to the changing environment in which it finds itself.

The same is true for brands. Whether your brand lives or dies will be dictated by how you evolve, and if you evolve at all.

A brand is a living thing. Once you launch, you begin to test and learn. You figure out what works and what doesn't, and you adapt.

Consistency and repetition are key for brand salience, but adaptability is key for customer connection. Knowing when to evolve and how to evolve is tricker.

Let's look at three distinct tactics.

The Complete Overhaul: Oatly

Ten years ago, many would have rolled their eyes at the idea of turning oats into milk and dismissed the product as something only for sensitive-stomached sissies or health nuts.

Now an oat milk latte is the second most common beverage of choice at many Australian cafes. In our office, it's the most common coffee order.

And Swedish company Oatly have had a lot to do with this.

When the brand first launched in the early 1990s, sales were slow and then flat.

In 2014, CEO Toni Petersson came in and turned the brand on its head with one of the best rebrands we've seen.

He hired a creative team and ensured they were involved in every aspect of the business, from product development to packaging design.

First, they recognised that the target market needed to expand from just lactose-intolerant people to anyone who drinks milk. This meant shifting the messaging to a broader benefit; emphasising its environmental benefits compared to dairy milk.

They adopted the philosophy 'Be human, not a logo', and they got work completely overhauling the brand.

The packaging became their billboard, filled with bold type and conversational language. The company changed its logo from a small red 'Oatly' in the corner to a bold, block letter 'OAT-LY!' at the front. They used an irreverent, anti-institutional tone of voice with controversial slogans like, 'It's like milk, but made for humans' and 'The post-milk generation'.

Their packaging copy included a space that read, 'Another side of our packaging providing no reason at all why you should try this product.'

They lived and breathed the disruptor brand mentality.

In 2021, Oatly went public with a valuation of $10 billion.

KEY LESSON: Commit to the schtick.
OTHER BRANDS TO LOOK AT: Old Spice, Athletic Greens.

The Subtle Evolution: Coca-Cola

When we set out to write this book, we said we wouldn't use typical brands for case studies. But, when it comes to branding, few names are as iconic – or as carefully managed – as Coca-Cola. Recognised instantly in over 200 countries, the red and white logo is more than just a brand; it's a piece of culture.

But what many people don't realise is that Coca-Cola has *rebranded* dozens of times. Every few years, the company makes small refinements to its logo, typography and packaging. The changes are so slight that most consumers barely notice: a smoothing of the cursive script, a gentle tweak to the proportions, a softening of the wave in their unique 'Dynamic Ribbon Device'.

And that's very intentional. For a brand with such deep emotional resonance, a radical overhaul would risk alienating generations of loyal customers. A full rebrand – a new logo, new colour palette or a complete departure – would cause public outcry and almost certainly damage sales. Coca-Cola understands that their brand equity is rooted not just in familiarity, but in the comfort and nostalgia the brand evokes.

Instead of revolution, Coca-Cola opts for subtle *evolution*. They modernise their brand just enough to stay relevant – refreshing packaging to suit contemporary tastes, adjusting to different markets or updating brand campaigns to reflect current culture – all while preserving the visual identity that's been consistent for over 130 years.

KEY LESSON: A rebrand doesn't always have to be loud to be effective.
OTHER BRANDS TO LOOK AT: Google, BMW.

The Hark Back to Heritage: Burberry

In 2023, Daniel Lee took over as Chief Creative Officer at Burberry and recognised an opportunity – not to chase a modern, minimal look and feel, but to return to what made Burberry distinct in the first place. He reintroduced one of the brand's oldest emblems: the Equestrian Knight Design, first created in 1901. The knight, bearing a flag with the word 'Prorsum' (Latin for 'forward'), symbolised progress, craftsmanship and British pride – the very DNA of Burberry.

Alongside the revived icon, Lee debuted a new serif wordmark inspired by archival typefaces, replacing the modern, sans serif logo. It was a bold countermove at a time when most luxury brands were modernising their identities. Lee leaned into tradition, but gave it new life: the branding was rolled out through campaigns that celebrated Britishness, shot against iconic London backdrops and styled with a contemporary eye, but were firmly rooted in the brand's heritage.

This return to roots wasn't nostalgia for nostalgia's sake. It was strategic. In a world where brands were starting to look and sound the same, Burberry's return to its historic aesthetic gave it distinctiveness. It reinforced what made the brand *Burberry* – not just another luxury house, but an emblem of British legacy, craftsmanship and innovation.

KEY LESSON: Sometimes you need to go back to go forwards.
OTHER BRANDS TO LOOK AT: Kodak.

Willow & Blake's Brand Evolution

When it came time to update the Willow & Blake brand, we kicked that can down the road over and over again. The irony of being in branding is that you're so busy building everyone else's brands that you neglect your own.

Our brand had grown stale, our website was seldom refreshed and there were actual tumbleweeds where there should have been content on our socials.

So naturally, as founders, we decided in one moment that this was the most important thing to focus on. After years of our teams telling us they were too busy for the briefs, we made the time. Funny how that works. Within eight weeks, we designed and deployed a new brand and website that kept the best elements of the Willow & Blake brand and softened those that had been overpowering for too long. Our new website showcased our work, and our updated social media strategy and content saw us grow our account by over 15,000 people in less than a year with no paid advertising and one or two posts per week.

It wasn't rocket science. It was a set of small adjustments and holding ourselves accountable when we didn't do what we said we would.

First, we said goodbye to the girl who had defined our first decade. Then we said 'tone it down' to the green that was overpowering us. Then it was goodbye to us (the founders) almost entirely, and hello to our work finally taking place front and centre. These changes made huge impacts on the agency, the last one in particular helping a whole new crop of established brands see us in a different light. As a result, the calibre of clients we work with changed literally overnight.

When You Know You Need to Rebrand

Where to start

Some parts of a brand's evolution will occur naturally. You add a new SKU and need a new colour; or you're shooting a new campaign, and your old art direction is looking tired so you try something different.

Some will be more practical. Maybe your old brand guardrails are no longer serving you. Your hero colour poses a legibility issue, or your typography isn't readable across multiple formats.

And sometimes, a brand's evolution will be a lifeline. Your sales are declining or flat; you're failing to acquire new customers; or your competitors are taking your market share.

The way to approach a rebrand or a brand evolution is very different to how you should approach creating a brand from scratch.

The first stage is deciding what the objective is. This should be a strategic decision, not an emotional one. Go back to the roots of the brand to decide what elements are fundamental to the brand and should be protected at all costs, and what elements are open to evolution. Often, we need to look at what is still relevant and what has dated and is no longer relevant.

We have a handy graph we use at Willow & Blake to help our clients make rebranding decisions. This was passed onto us by Brent Vrdoljak, who found it in a study by the Ehrenberg-Bass Institute in the US. Summarised, this graph articulates that you only want to keep the assets of your brand that are unique and identifiable.

A key strategy we like to use is dialling up your key brand attributes. Take frank, for example – one of unique brand attributes is our tone of voice and cheeky copy. So, when we updated our packaging, we made the copy supersized. It's the first thing you read. We also homed in on our hero colour (pink) and elevated the brand with more premium packaging details like subtle foiling.

It's important to note that a rebrand or brand evolution is not just updating your logo, typography and colourways. It's updating every element of your brand from the positioning to the tone of voice, the imagery to the packaging. Ensuring consistency across every consumer touchpoint is key.

How to understand your current position

Start with your current customers – the loyal ones who have been with you from the beginning and the new ones who you want to attract more of.

This can be as simple as surveys segmented by purchasing habits and as detailed as in-person interviews. You want to identify the key elements they associate with your brand.

Then you want to look at the wider population. This is arguably even more important than your existing customers, particularly if your challenge is acquisition.

This is best done through third-party brand tracking. We use a platform called Tracksuit that makes brand tracking simple and beautiful. (Disclaimer for transparency – we are investors in Tracksuit.)

The key elements we always look at are whether people think 'this is a brand for me,' based on their age, and a word map that tells us what words the general population associate with your brand.

This can be very eye-opening for brands, because we tend to live in echo chambers. When you live and breathe a brand, you assume everyone does. Realistically, most people don't think about your brand. And if they do, it's for less than five seconds while they are deciding if it's a brand for them or not.

If the words people are associating with your brand are not the words you want associated with your brand, it's time to change something.

For example, frank body's origin story was heavily rooted in coffee. We are known for the Original Coffee Scrub. We launched in a cafe. For years, it was our hook: frank equals coffee, coffee equals frank.

Ten years later, though, our ingredient philosophy has evolved and become a lot more sophisticated. We moved from coffee-based skin care into high-performance body care, and ingredients like glycolic acid are much more prevalent now in our SKUs.

However, when we looked at how the wider population perceived us, 'coffee' was a key word that came up again and again. This indicated we had an education issue, and we needed to raise awareness of our other products.

Our marketing department took this insight and developed a new strategy starting with a campaign whereby for a whole month we talked about nothing but our Glycolic Body Scrub. The results? It became our bestseller, and the audience started to associate the brand with high-performance body care as opposed to coffee.

Use the insights you find to form your strategy.

An important point here is to take insights from your consumers but don't let consumer testing rule your creative decision-making.

It's now easier than ever to get feedback on your branding. Consumer testing platforms have popped up all over the internet and in less than a day you can A/B test logos, packaging and taglines. But should you?

No. Brands need to define their own position in the market. If we let the masses decide, we'll end up in a sea of sameness.

Execute the strategy

Depending on the significance of the rebrand and the relationship you have with your customers, there are two ways to do this. You can take your customer on a journey, or you can rip the Band-Aid off.

Just remember: opinions are like arseholes. Everyone is going to have one.

There are numerous cases of rebrands that have resulted in public outcry: Harry's, The Daily Edited.

If your strategy is sound, you must commit. People don't like change. Take comfort in the fact that at least they care enough about your brand to notice the change. It will take time to rebuild the memory structures your consumers had with the old look and feel. But stay consistent, stay on brand and it will be worth it.

frank body would not be where it is today if we had kept those kraft bags.

Betts: A modern Australian legacy

On homing in on a brand identity

Founded in 1892 by Fanny Breckler, Betts is one of Australia's longest standing shoe empires – a fifth-generation family business built on craft, creativity and care. Betts has survived by evolving time and time again and is a household name synonymous with quality, comfort and family values. In early 2025, Jess was approached by Betts to help them work out what their next move was. The brand had evolved, perhaps too much, with a web of sub-brands, products and customer categories making the overall offering confusing. At the heart of it all was a great womenswear collection led by a talented design team who knew how to produce fashion-forward shoes for women with a premium finish and affordable price point.

Beyond that, Betts had a deep history that most fashion brands would die for. This was the sweet spot to own: Betts is where heritage and history meet contemporary style. Betts waved goodbye to men's, kids' and the various sub-brands – homing in on a well-crafted offering for the modern woman. Next, Betts needed a brand that reflected the quality of their product and the next era of this proudly family-operated business. That's where Willow & Blake stepped in.

The new logo, set in Bodoni, embodies both legacy and modernity. The icon is the letter B several times over, representing the family gathered around the table where every decision is made. The typography treatment is aligned to luxury fashion, and elevated packaging becomes a distinctive asset – leaving the shopping centre proudly with your Betts oxblood bag. The art direction and creative storytelling all ladders up from the creative platform Classic with a Twist. It strikes the balance between timeless and trend-aware – it's mainstream enough to feel familiar, yet artful enough to spark intrigue.

We elevated the brand voice to speak directly to the modern woman – confident, conversational and charmingly off-beat. The mixed-idiom wordplay reflects a brand created by one big strappy family. Alongside new fitouts rolling out across flagship stores, we also created a clean, intuitive website and an artful social strategy to bring Betts to life online.

Shareable, saveable content, tastemaker collaborations and a consistent, creative aesthetic make the brand feel familiar and trusted, yet fresh and exciting. It's classic, with a twist. At the time of writing, the rebrand has been live in market for four months, and the public reception has been fantastic, with key metrics all starting to turn in the right direction.

Summary of tips

- Evolve or die
- Be strategic, not emotional
- Amplify key brand cues
- Commit and stay consistent

THE LESSON:

It's right there in the title of this chapter – evolve or die.

Chapter 15

CAPITAL CONTROL

Jess was the one answering the question. She had the context, she had the data, she had the ideas, yet the investor refused to look at her. To acknowledge that she, a mere woman, may be the one with the answer to the problem was too much for his pea-sized brain to comprehend. Welcome to the world of capital raising.

Throughout our journey, our emails were aflutter with notes from venture capitalists, private equity and strategic investors from all corners of the globe. The underlying message: we want to give you money. It was an alluring offer for a few broke writers who had resigned themselves to the fact that due to our career choices we were unlikely to ever own homes. Oh, the things we wish we could go back and tell those naive versions of ourselves.

And so began what we called the girl band tour: countless flights, meetings on the 74th floor overlooking Central Park, Trafalgar Square, Boston Square, the 7th arrondissement. We clocked up and used frequent flyer miles like there was no tomorrow, because in our minds, there really *may* not have been a tomorrow. That's the reality of a small, fledgling business.

The truth is that we had no idea what we were doing. We had zero experience in the world of mergers and acquisitions (M&A), no formal advisors and no clue. We took Zoom calls, phone calls and lunch dates to chat, learn, absorb and decide. We wasted weeks' worth of time in conversations that were going nowhere because we didn't know what we wanted. Over the years, we honed a set of finely sharpened skills when it comes to capital raising, but like all things, that learning came at a cost. And not just a monetary one.

The world of M&A is like the Wild West, but instead of chaps they wear expensively tailored suits and instead of guns they sling NBIOs (non-binding indicative offers).

In an industry full of snakes, we have been lucky to come across a handful of extremely decent, well intentioned, value-aligned people whom we have called on for their input into this book. The goal of this chapter is to give you a crash course in capital raising with the headline advice being: *find a good advisor before you do anything.*

There are five types of capital:

- Bootstrapping: Using your own money and revenue to fund growth. Most DTC brands start here.
- Angel investment: Early-stage funding from high-net-worth individuals, often ranging from $25,000 to $250,000.
- Venture capital: Larger institutional investments, typically starting at $1 million, focused on high-growth potential.
- Private equity: Later-stage investment, usually for established brands with significant revenue ($10 million plus).
- Strategic investment: Investment from larger companies in your industry, often leading to acquisition.

There are multiple ways you can get capital and give equity:

- SAFE notes: 'SAFE' stands for Simple Agreement for Future Equity; an investment popular with early-stage startups.
- Convertible notes: Debt that converts to equity, common in seed rounds.
- Preferred shares: A standard venture capital investment vehicle with special rights.
- Common shares: Basic equity without special preferences.
- Debt financing: An alternative to equity, becoming more popular in the DTC space.

Raising Capital: A Strategic Checklist

Before you start seeking investment, work through these key considerations:

1. Define your 'why'
    - What specific growth challenges are you trying to solve?
    - Could these challenges be solved without external capital?

2. What are your objectives?
    - What do you want to achieve in the next twelve months?
    - Where do you see the business in two or three years?
    - What's your long-term vision beyond five years?

3. What are your exact funding requirements?
    - Have you created a detailed budget?
    - How long will this funding last?
    - Have you added a 20 per cent buffer for unexpected costs?

4. How will you use the money?
    - Where exactly will the funds be allocated?
    - Are these goals what you really want for your business?
    - How will they change your role, your team and your profitability?

5. What are you prepared to offer?
    - How much equity are you willing to give up?
    - Will you offer board positions?
    - What voting rights will investors have? (Hot tip: they will largely decide this, but you should know where your line is.)
    - What's your expected exit strategy?

6. Who is your ideal investor?
    - What industry knowledge should they have?
    - What connections do you need?
    - How can they help guide the business?
    - Do their values match yours?

7. What else do you need besides funding?
    - What mentorship would help you grow?
    - What operational help do you require?
    - What market opportunities are you seeking?

Remember: The right investor at the wrong time is the wrong investor. Take time to thoroughly work through this checklist before starting conversations.

There are generally three major players involved in each transaction: the founder, the advisor and the investor. We sat down with each one to give you the inside look.

The investor

Michael Da Gama Pinto – founding partner, Era VC/ former CFO, Swisse

Throughout the course of raising capital for two companies, becoming angel investors ourselves, introducing clients to trusted advisors and generally trying to become as educated as possible on all things M&A, we met Michael Da Gama Pinto. Mike is the founding partner of Era VC – which boasts a portfolio of brands such as WelleCo, Seed and Conserving Beauty – and is also the former Chief Financial Officer of Swisse. He is a good person and he knows a lot about money, which is a rare combination. We asked him some questions about what investors are looking for in brands now so that you can learn firsthand how to build and position a consumer brand for investment.

Mike, can you sum up your investment philosophy for us in a few sentences?

We back visionary founders – those truly looking to redefine the categories in which they operate. We look to be supportive partners and that comes in many forms. Of course, access to capital is part of that, but equally we act as a sounding board for the team, help sort out distribution or supply chain niggles and offer financial expertise.

Personally, I love to work with founders who want to do the right thing by their customers day in, day out. This isn't always the easiest path, but we believe it builds enduring legacies that compound over time.

We look to support brands that will leave legacies that thrive long beyond our involvement.

What attributes are you looking for in businesses you invest in?

Intangibles: A business with a clear reason to exist; one that cares deeply for its customers and employees, and consistently delivers on its brand promise. It earns trust through product efficacy, builds loyalty over time and lays the foundation for something that can endure for decades.

Tangibles: A business with a business model that allows it to control its cash (i.e. knows when to raise, when to acquire debt or generate its own cash). This usually means it has a gross margin profile that allows enough profit after acquiring its next customer.

What attributes are you looking for in the founders you invest in?

Intangibles: Brave. Visionary. Storytellers. Fiercely passionate teachers who are obsessed about their customers and driven to create meaningful change.

Tangibles: Founders willing to do the hard things and lead by example. Calculated risk-takers who know when to accelerate or slow down.

What do you believe people spend too much time worrying about during fundraising that isn't really that important?

Founders often obsess over past financial performance, trends to be derived from this and what that means for the future. From our perspective, of course, understanding your own business data and KPIs is exceptionally important for the day-to-day operations, and for near-term planning, but for the longer term, the best founders we work with have the ability to balance today with a clear expectation and path to future growth. They also have the ability to tell that story and get buy-in from employees, suppliers, retailers and investors about the potential of the brand, and that affords them access to opportunities that others don't have.

When we're looking at investments, past performance educates us on what to expect in the near future, but the more confidence you can give an investor (or potential acquirer) about the future (contracts, customer testimonials, growth opportunities) the more value can be attributed to the business today.

Often founders and investors spend too much time focused on current year performance, but an investor or acquirer is normally buying the next three to ten years of profit or cashflow and this is where the focus needs to be.

Vice versa, what do people often overlook?

We've learned from our own mistakes – founders often get hooked on a headline valuation for their business when chatting to investors and we go through cycles of having to pay higher prices for businesses than we might like. I can't stress enough, this never ends well for founders or investors. It puts so much pressure on a founder to deliver in the short term that often decisions that are better for the longer term are overlooked or compromised. It's really hard for us as investors to have a long-term perspective with this in mind, so it shouldn't be overlooked that for both parties, higher valuations now aren't always better. It can take decades to build an enduring brand but in overpaying going in the focus for founders and investors is on quickly maximising the value short term, which is never beneficial.

We've also learned that it's virtually impossible for founders to 'outgrow' poor decisions early on, either with rushing to find a co-founder or early foundational hires. If you get these wrong, no amount of investment will make the business work. Cohesion of the team and fundamental business culture can't come from a nice deck or agency spiel. It must be lived and breathed by all your early hires. Without that cohesion, you'll struggle to move through the hard times as well as the good.

What advice can you provide first-time capital raisers to ensure they get a fair and equitable deal?

Founders have to be true to themselves about what they want to build and their aspirations for the business. 'Fair and equitable' has many meanings, but should present a good base from which to scale. The highest price isn't always the best partner. Trust your gut when you meet potential partners, because you'll be working alongside them for a long time. Go into any process with a clear sense of what you want to achieve and what your top priorities are – it might be ownership stake, it might be having certain help around the table. All mean different things for different deals. Of course, competitive tension between parties is helpful in understanding whether you're getting a fair and equitable deal as you can benchmark different terms and valuations, but always look carefully at the small print – funds can hide some nasties in there!

Remember that any investment discussion is a courtship on both sides, and a bidder is never nicer to you than in the first term sheet. This is your time for negotiation, and it's critical you surround yourself with trusted experts to guide you through this. If you can't get the change you need then, it's very unlikely to come later.

What should founders expect from the capital raising process?

It's brutal, although it does get easier each time you do it.

It is very hard to run your own business, act as a leader and inspiration to the team, hit the numbers you have put in your financial forecast, *and* then show up each day with a smile on your face to answer different variations of the same question from each investor.

It's critical to understand that this is a unique experience in your life and surround yourself with help. Some founders wind up loving it and leaning in, and some see it as a necessary part of building their business. But understand what motivates you to get through it, because once you've brought on investors, you're likely to have to do it more than once.

It's also important to keep reminding yourself of *why* you are raising capital. Often you are doing it to accelerate your businesses prospects (above solely cashflow funding it) so that acceleration decision is likely to come with some upfront pain – often in the form of lots of meetings and due diligence.

What do you believe founders should look for in an advisor and in their final investment partner?

Investment will always take longer and be harder than you think. You have to be okay working with these people through thick and thin. If you can't imagine calling them in the bad times as well as the good then they're probably not the right partner for you. If an investor isn't aligned on what you want to build and what success looks like, it's not a fit. Just walk away – your life will be a constant battle if you don't agree on the end goal.

Whether you're looking for an advisor to help you get investment or sell your business, you should choose someone with experience in your industry. Research at least the last ten transactions in your industry and talk to the advisors whose names appear most.

Relationships matter. You want an advisor who can call up an acquirer or investor in your field of choice and have their call answered. Advisors who understand how your acquirer thinks are invaluable to you. A good advisor becomes the interface between you and a bidder and can often improve your position and limit the damage to your future working relationship with your partner or acquirer.

Any final words of wisdom?

Enjoy the build. You can be in a rush to get to exit, but while there are some additional financial freedoms that come from the exit I know so many (myself included) who regret never fully enjoying the build phase.

Most importantly, run your own race. Block out noise about where you think you should be and just focus on the right things, at the right time with the right people. It's far more satisfying and rewarding than the alternative.

The founder

Jessica Hatzis and Bree Johnson – co-founders, frank body and Willow & Blake

Now it's time for our perspective as founders on what we loved and loathed about the capital raising process. We interviewed each other for this section.

Capital raising: we have much to say about this topic, but how would you summarise your experience in one word?

J: Turbulent.
B: Complicated.

What do you wish someone had told you before you raised capital?

J: How much preference shares will come back to bite you in the arse.
B: No one is going to grow your business but you. And be aware of the terms on convertible notes.

What would you do differently in the future?

J: I'm not a huge believer in redoing things; I believe we learn valuable lessons even in the hardest and most frustrating of times. I would, however, speak up more – I didn't always voice what was important to me and that came back to hurt me tenfold down the track.

B: Overall, we've had very supportive investors. But I think you get out what you put in. In the future, I would ask for more and report less. More questions, more connections and more advice.

What have been the greatest benefits of raising capital in your businesses?

J: Honestly, it has little to do with moving the needle in the business and more to do with my own (now relatively robust) financial knowledge, which was almost entirely lacking before. That is priceless.

B: Funding our retail and regional expansion, pushing us to grow up as a business and as leaders, accountability.

A chat with Charlie Gearside - co-founder, Eucalyptus

Building your wealth over time through sweat equity

Charlie Gearside is the co-founder of Eucalyptus, a health tech startup responsible for brands such as Pilot and Kin. He was previously the Creative Director of Koala, one of our favourite brand references for esoteric and irreverent branding and campaigns in an otherwise dull category. Charlie is a proponent of sweat equity - whereby you work in exchange for a percentage of ownership in a company - being a great way for people to create their own wealth beyond a regular salary. Because, as we millennials know all too well, salaries do not grow anywhere near at the rate of inflation, meaning that those with generational wealth leap further and further ahead and those without it struggle to ever imagine owning a home. As two writers who believed we would never be able to afford our own houses, we can attest to the fact that ownership of an asset, even though money was not the primary driver, has been crucial in establishing ourselves financially. For many people, talking about money is taboo. It felt that way for us, too. Now we realise that talking about it is necessary, especially to help those in marginalised communities have a better chance at evening the scales. Charlie has experience in both receiving and giving sweat equity, so we asked him a few questions to help you.

Charlie, you call sweat equity the last great opportunity in Australia for people to create real wealth and we agree. Could you explain this concept and the options available to people?

Sweat equity is trading your time, energy and skill for ownership instead of just a salary. It's what I did. I didn't come from money, didn't go to uni, but I threw myself into building something and took equity over cash. That decision changed my life.

In Australia, the traditional wealth paths like property and super aren't working for most people anymore. If you want to get ahead, you need to own something. Sweat equity is one of the last ways to do that without already being rich. It's a source of social mobility.

Sweat equity is not just for founders. Designers, engineers, marketers, operators – anyone who can help build a business can take sweat equity. The trick is finding a place where your work really moves the needle, and the ownership on offer actually means something.

What are some lessons you would provide to founders considering giving equity to their team?

Don't be tight. Equity is a trust signal. If you want people to act like owners, actually make them owners. Too many founders hoard equity like it's Gollum's ring. But holding onto it too tightly doesn't help you build faster. Grow the pie and be okay with a slightly smaller slice.

Most people don't understand equity. They hear 'shares' and think it's a guaranteed payday. You need to explain how it works – vesting, dilution, what the shares actually represent. The more transparent you are, the more aligned your team will be.

What advice would you give to someone wanting to position themselves for sweat equity?

Go where you can have an impact. That usually means early-stage companies where things are still being built and every contribution matters. Don't chase the highest salary until your late thirties. Instead, chase learning, influence and a clear path to ownership.

And ask for it. Just say, 'I want to be aligned with the success of this business. If I can help grow it, I'd love to share in the upside.' If that's a weird conversation for the founder, you're probably in the wrong room.

Also, do your homework. Ask how much equity is on the table, how many shares are already issued, what the valuation is and what the long-term plan is. You don't need to be a finance expert, but you do need to understand what you're signing up for.

What conversations should an employer and employee be having who are considering entering this type of relationship?

Think of it like a work version of a prenup. It's a bit awkward at first, but it avoids way bigger problems later. Ask questions like:

- What kind of equity is being offered – shares or options – and how do they vest?
- How much equity is on offer, and what does that mean as a percentage of the company?
- What happens if either side wants out early?
- Is there a clear growth plan or exit strategy?
- How is fundraising going?

You don't need to get lost in legal detail, but both sides need to be clear on expectations. Misalignment at the start can blow things up later.

Any other words of advice?

Don't wait for permission.

The traditional playbook just doesn't work anymore. The people who are getting ahead are taking bets, building leverage and owning outcomes. Sweat equity is one of the few ways left to turn effort into real upside. So be useful. Learn fast. Take a risk. Get on the cap table.

Don't just build someone else's dream for a paycheck. Make sure you get a piece of it.

THE LESSON:

Money talks, so you need to talk about money.

Chapter 16

CELEBRATING THE HIGHS

Party in Your Birthday Suit

It's a universal truth that whenever you throw a birthday party there comes a moment when you think, 'What if no one shows up?'

Maybe you're six and you've invited the whole of Year 1 to your unicorn ice cream party and you're begging your mum to confirm she did indeed send out the invites. Or you're twenty-seven and you've spent half of your brand's marketing budget on a pop-up shop to celebrate your birthday and you're really hoping people come.

Willow & Blake was built on celebrations: we knew community and word of mouth would be instrumental in getting our little agency off the ground, so we threw purposeful parties that brought together creatives from all over Melbourne and gave them themes, such as the 'Fuck Love' party we threw on Valentine's Day. Building community offline was and still is just as important as the digital communities marketers obsess over.

Now we continue to run key events for Willow & Blake, but they are very different; more refined, more educational, positioning the agency as a thought leader in the world of consumer brands. A recent event we ran titled 'How Women Shop' brought together founders from some of Australia's best fashion and retail brands to listen to a panel that included us and Edwina McCann, Editor of Vogue Australia. Little Jess and Bree of yesteryear, throwing parties in laneways with boxes of cider we'd coordinated in exchange for copywriting services would never have believed it could happen. But it's a testament to starting where you are, playing to your strengths at the time and evolving as you can. And always believing in your why.

At frank body, in-person celebrations took place less often due to the online nature of our business. However, we were determined to find ways to stay connected with our community and share the wins with them.

For frank body's fifth birthday, we created our first retail experience. We wanted to give back to our customers, so rather than a flashy influencer or media event, we decided to throw a party for our community with a pop-up shop. The best part? Everything was free.

We created a pink fantasy land on Chapel Street complete with a sushi-train–style conveyer belt that rotated through our old favourites, new products and exclusive custom-made merchandise we'd created in collaboration with local designer Ellen Porteus.

It was a two-day pop-up, but the build had been extensive. We wanted to impress and so we'd invested in creating everything custom for the space.

The outside of the building was wrapped in pink decals that read 'Party in your birthday suit'. A frank body light box hung above the door. You couldn't see inside, which obviously made everyone want to see inside.

Once you did, you were greeted with a barrage of our signature pink Pantone and red, a custom colour we'd chosen for this campaign. There were shelves of carefully merchandised products. A curvy mirror ready to oblige a thousand selfies.

But the crème de la crème was the custom-made pink sushi train with fluffy pink seats.

We'd been promoting the pop-up to our 700,000+-strong Instagram community for weeks, sent out the EDMs, and done the press.

But even so, as we met up an hour before the doors opened on the first day, we were nervous. We drove down from the office together in Jess's car, both wearing the custom jumpers we'd had designed. Jess wore hers with jeans; Bree with a black skirt.

As we neared the venue, we saw it: a line.

Not just any line. A line that snaked around the corner. A line of people waiting to get into our pop-up an hour before it opened. We squealed as we jumped up and down hugging each other.

Across the road, we heard people saying, 'That's Jess and Bree – the founders. I hope they say hi'. We were ecstatic that they even knew who we were. We got to work meeting our customers. We went up and down the line delivering free coffees, hugs and even took a few selfies.

As a predominately ecommerce brand, we didn't often get to see our customers in the wild unless we brought them together on purpose, or stood in front of our retail gondolas like total creeps. So, to meet them in this way was pure joy.

It was these people – our customers and community – that made the brand a success.

Three Takeaways from All the Celebrations, Community Gatherings and Events We Have Run Over the Years

- **YOUR COMMUNITY IS YOUR BIGGEST ASSET; TREAT THEM LIKE VIPS.** The magic has always been in making our customers feel seen and celebrated. When you build a brand that gives more than it takes – whether it's free coffee, a photo moment, or genuine connection – people show up for you. Literally.

- **NEVER UNDERESTIMATE THE POWER OF SHOWING UP IN PERSON.** Digital brands often forget that their community doesn't just live online. Seeing faces, hearing firsthand experiences, seeing who buys your product. The energy of that line down Chapel Street for frank body's first pop-up? You can't buy that with ads.

- **THE NERVES NEVER GO AWAY AND THAT'S A GOOD THING.** That 'what if no one shows up' fear keeps you humble. It means you still care. Every founder feels it – even founders of a global brand. The key is to do it anyway. That mix of excitement and terror is proof you're building something worth showing up for.

THE LESSON:

Pause.
Celebrate.
You will need those good moments to get you through all the hard ones.

Chapter 17

THE MOTHERLOAD

Our stories, like many mothers' stories, are layered and complex.

For Bree, motherhood is a constant rebrand – one that never really settles. It's equal parts identity crisis and awakening, exhaustion and euphoria. You spend years defining yourself by what you do – the job title, the business, the achievements – and then a baby arrives, and everything that once felt foundational suddenly feels small.

It's confronting to realise how much of your self-worth was tied to your work, to the nods of approval when people heard what you did: 'Founder'; 'Director'. And then almost overnight those words feel irrelevant. You're someone's mum now. The validation fades, replaced by something quieter but infinitely deeper.

The early days blur together: the visitors, the flowers, the milk-stained tops. The bleeding, the crying, the nights that never end. The emails that still come through, the Slack messages you half-read with a newborn asleep on your chest. The guilt for wanting to stay connected. The guilt for not wanting to.

Work never completely leaves your mind, especially if it once defined you. But something inside shifts. The drive softens. Ambition takes on a new shape. The version of you who once sprinted toward every goal now moves slower, deliberately. You begin to understand that there's strength in stillness, too.

Then comes the return – the complicated middle ground. You find that you're not quite the person you were, but you're also not yet comfortable in who you've become. The world has moved on; the inbox is full; the baby is sick again. You fake it until the fog lifts, until one day you realise you're back – not the same, but stronger, steadier.

Motherhood doesn't erase ambition; it reorders it. And just when you think you have it sorted, motherhood will throw you a speed hump to keep you on your toes.

You learn to let go of expectations, of perfection, of timelines. You build a village. You outsource the chaos. You stop apologising for needing help. You forgive yourself for missing bedtimes and for loving your work. You bring your kids to your office and let your worlds collide.

And somewhere in between the work calls and the cuddles, the versions of you – founder, mother, partner, friend – start to coexist. Messily, beautifully, humanly. You're no longer one thing. You're everything, all at once.

Motherhood doesn't ask you to give up who you are. It just asks you to become more of it.

At the time of writing this, Bree has two beautiful boys. She's frustrated that the world is not set up to support working parents, but is pleased to report she still believes you can have it all – just not at the same time.

Jess's experience was different.

In the last six years she's miscarried once, had one C-section, one vaginal birth and now has two beautiful girls earthside with her.

Morning sickness had Jess vomiting in the bin before running out the door to deliver a keynote right after world-renowned professor Scott

Galloway. She sat in the office bathroom crying after getting her period, realising she wasn't pregnant. She's walked out of a staff performance review due to her doctor calling with results about what would eventually become the loss of her first pregnancy. She's turned up at the office like nothing happened forty-eight hours after losing that baby. She breastfed her first child through board meetings and read 200-page legal documents with a weeks-old baby in the carrier.

Jess did all of this while managing two growing companies, going through three successful capital raises, exiting key staff, launching new products, and weathering global pandemics and economic recessions. Alongside all of that – keeping all those balls in the air while having nausea twenty-four hours a day, pregnancy insomnia, colicky newborns, breastfeeding, birth recovery and the demands of toddlers – she *still* doubted herself.

Jess felt guilty about every decision she made. She thought she was never giving enough, doing enough or being enough. She felt like she had to be everyone and be everything to everyone. However, giving every last ounce of energy she had to others meant that there was absolutely nothing left for herself.

One day, in mid-2024, while Jess's youngest was a mere eight weeks old, she decided enough was enough. This simply couldn't go on. She remembered that she started her own businesses so that she could define life on her own terms and she intended to do that every single day going forward.

Jess realised she had nothing to prove to the world and that she needed to stop chasing validation from others about how she parented or worked, because that is a never-ending pursuit. This is a privilege not afforded to most mothers – and that is something that we collectively need to change.

Before Having Kids

For many founders and self-employed women, going on parental leave means either turning off your income stream so you can pay someone else to do your job or not really taking parental leave.

In Australia, 79 per cent of mums who took leave to care for their child returned to work within twelve months, and 79 per cent said they would have liked to have taken more leave. This timeframe is often much shorter for self-employed women, who are usually the face of the brand and are personally responsible for ensuring the company keeps running, can pay its staff and bills and service clients.

When we began our businesses in our early twenties, the concept of parental leave wasn't even on our radar. We were much more concerned with how we would afford our vodka, lime and sodas on the weekend than how our future selves would juggle owning a business and raising tiny humans.

But as our carefree twenties came to an end and our married friends started to procreate, we decided to sit down for a very honest conversation about our plans. We recognised that both of us wanted kids at some stage in the next five to ten years and that we needed to start planning for that now. Kudos to us for being so forward-thinking.

The first step was to start a savings account to put away money so we could pay ourselves maternity leave. We knew we both wanted to have the option of staying home for a period of time. We worked very hard in our twenties to earn enough money so that we could have the option. Many families work just as hard and don't have the option.

In Australia, the government does offer paid parental leave based on the weekly rate of the national minimum wage. In 2025, this was $183.16 a day before tax, or $915.80 per five-day week.

Companies in Australia can top this pay up or offer their own employees paid parental leave schemes. But as a founder, it's more complicated than ensuring you have enough cash flow to cover your wage. Your role is hard to replace.

Hard, but not impossible.

For us, finding replacements looked like a combination of restructuring and mat leave covers at both Willow & Blake and frank body. At Willow & Blake, we brought on a general manager to keep the ship steady while we both took time off. He bought into the business and ran it for over seven years. We will be forever grateful to him for that.

Our plan had been to try to tag-team our pregnancies, but nature has a way of making her own rules and we ended up pregnant at the same time. Jess with her first and Bree with her second. We made quite the pair, bumping around the office joking about going into labour in the board room.

It was beautiful to have that experience together as best friends, but slightly terrifying for us as business owners. We've always joked that we are one brain, and the way we've been able to juggle two businesses for so long is that we can seamlessly integrate into each other's role and pick up where they left off.

As brand custodians, what would happen when we both weren't there to protect the integrity of the brand? Who would be the customer's voice? Who would say, 'No, it's not up to scratch – do it again'?

It turned out that the team managed fine without us. Everything was not done exactly as we would have done it, but it was done.

Over a period of six years, we have both had two beautiful children each. Jess has two girls: Ellery and Daisy. Bree has two boys: Ned and Hugo.

We both took maternity leave twice: Bree for nine months with Ned and six months with Hugo; Jess for six months with Ellery and twelve months with Daisy.

Maternity leave is different for every working mum. Yes, ours was filled with board meetings we had to breastfeed through; HR crises that meant we used precious nap times for meetings when we too should have been sleeping; capital raises that coincided with contractions; and way too many lengthy and heavy contracts read and signed while bouncing a baby in a carrier.

But it was worth it. While we both get a lot of purpose and fulfilment from work, nothing compares to our children. They are the best things we've ever created, and they give us more joy, happiness and pride than we could have ever imagined, simply by existing.

Going Back to Work (or Not)

Going back to work will look different for everyone, just like motherhood does.

Many founders and entrepreneurs never stop working, or they start their founder journey with their little ones already in the world. Some take extended leave. Some choose to not work outside the home again. There's no right or wrong.

Home and work are increasingly blurred with babies in the office and people working from home. This is a good thing. We strongly believe motherhood and business can coexist. However, we still need more support for working mothers. We need to talk about how we make work work.

The gender pay gap is still a big issue. In 2025, for every $1 a man earns, women earn 78 cents on average. A scarier fact than that is that women over fifty-five are the fastest-growing homeless demographic in Australia.

This is largely due to women not returning to the workforce after having children.

As a society, we need to do more to change these statistics.

How Motherhood Makes Better Leaders

Our children have given us many gifts. One of them is our ability to understand better what is and isn't a problem. Ending up in the emergency room because your twelve-month-old has COVID-related complications – that's a problem. A brief changing slightly, meaning you have to redo some elements of your work – not a huge problem. We learned how to prioritise, empathise, calm people down and get things done, because at the end of the day all we really want to do is maximise the time we can be present with our kids, making memories with them without forgoing what makes us who we are outside the home. Our definition of 'important' has changed, and so too has the work we spend our time doing. Work these days needs to have purpose – we have no interest in busy work anymore, and that has made us better founders, leaders and decision-makers.

Motherhood changes people – not just at home, but at work. Not in the polished, curated way often seen in leadership books, but in the real, messy way. Mothers come back to work different and often better.

Perspective

For many mothers, work used to feel huge. It was the most important thing in the world, and everything had to be perfect. Motherhood shrinks the scale of what counts as a crisis. Unless someone's bleeding or there's a real emergency, mothers don't spiral. They don't have the luxury. When you spend most of your life keeping another human alive, a client email just doesn't carry the same weight.

Time mastery

No one knows ruthless efficiency like a working mother on a deadline. When there's a hard stop at day care pick-up, there's no room for procrastination. Mothers learn to get more done in four hours than most people do in eight. They're focused, direct and no-fluff – because they have to be.

Resilience

Motherhood is an unpaid, unrelenting masterclass in how to operate through hard times.

Sleep deprivation is a literal torture technique used by the army. Mothers make decisions at 2am with crying babies on their chests. They learn to trust their guts when their brains are foggy. Their bodies are put through trauma. But they still get up and get it done every day.

Boundaries

The always-available girlboss is unlikely to survive motherhood. Mothers learn to draw harder lines. They work hard during the day because once they walk out the door, they're stepping into another full-time role. The hours between day care pick-up and bedtime are sacred. And ironically, the more boundaries mothers set, the more respect they command. This is good for their team and themselves.

Chaos tolerance

Motherhood is also a masterclass in managing chaos. Tantrums in public, fevers at midnight, school closures with no warning – it rewires the brain for flexibility. Mothers don't fear the unexpected; they expect it. In business, where plans rarely survive contact with reality, this ability is golden.

Empathy

Motherhood grows empathy in ways that leadership seminars can't teach. It's not performative. It's the kind of empathy that understands what it's like to run on two hours of sleep and coffee fumes. Mothers know people aren't machines – because they themselves aren't. They lead with more compassion and more humanity.

A Few Things We've Learned on This Wild Ride Called Motherhood

You can have it all – just not at the same time

We're the Spice Girl generation, raised on Girl Power – we were told to 'lean in', and that we could do and be anything. And we can – but we're also expected to work like we don't have kids and parent like we don't work.

These pressures are amplified by the echo chambers we live in. On TikTok, you see mothers creating lunch boxes that rival a Heston Blumenthal degustation while you stare at your sad Vegemite sandwich.

Every day is a balancing act. Saying yes to one thing means saying no to another. The tension between wanting to be present for your children and pursuing a fulfilling career never really disappears.

THE LESSON: The decision you make today can change tomorrow. It's okay to have multiple goals.

Not every day is a slay

We stole this one from Chelsea Morley, founder of Tiny Disco.

Some days, everything goes to shit. The nanny calls in sick, the baby won't sleep, you're late to day care pick-up. You get frustrated at work and snap at your toddler.

Give yourself grace. There's always time to turn a day around. If you can't make it to work, call in sick. Carer's leave exists for a reason. No one worth caring about will judge you – and if they do, that's their problem.

THE LESSON: Listen to your body, not just your head. It usually knows what you need. And if it's been a *really* bad day, call a friend – they'll have a story to match.

Men are carers too

Have honest conversations with your partner about dividing the load.

The 2024 National Working Families Survey found that while parental leave policies are improving, outdated gender roles persist.[31] Just 17 per cent of paid primary carers' leave is taken by men, according to the Workplace Gender Equality Agency Australia.[32]

Do better, men.

Sharing everything equally means both the mental load and the domestic labour. Weaponised incompetence is not acceptable.

THE LESSON: Find a partner who is a true partner.

Ask for help

Everyone's village looks different: child care, nannies, cleaners, assistants, family.

Use the resources you have and do what works for your family.

Bree is a big advocate for getting help – paid and unpaid. While her boys were young, she had a nanny two days a week, including a date night for her and her husband. The nanny cared not just for the boys but for the whole family; helping with laundry, changing sheets, picking up groceries. They eased the mental load and day-to-day chores to help the household run smoothly. Both Bree's sons did a mix of child care, nanny days and grandparent days. Bree knows she is privileged to afford this support, and as she works full-time, the support network allows her to truly focus on her kids when she's home.

THE BIGGEST LESSON:

Be a mother, not a motherfucker.

Chapter 18

GETTING COMFORTABLE WITH BEING UNCOMFORTABLE

Running a business is much like wearing a pair of six-inch stilettos all day, every day: to breakfast, to the gym, in the shower, to bed. There's no break, no relief and no time to let those little feet heal. It's just you and a box of Band-Aids trying to patch up the damage.

We don't say this to scare you, but rather to prepare you – because we weren't prepared for the demands of a fast-growing consumer brand and it caught us off guard. Learning to live with discomfort is the lesson every founder doesn't want but receives anyway. Class is officially in session, people. From people to product to profit and loss, the volatility is mostly unavoidable and the scrutiny (from others and from yourself) is real. frank body was a beast of its own making and we were thrust from copywriters to C-suite overnight with dozens of staff in Australia, the US, the UK and China, thousands of customers spanning to even further corners of the globe, a complex supply chain, cash flow constraints that come with growing a consumer brand into new regions and retailers and, of course, the leadership requirements that came with all of it. Suddenly we were in charge of much more than what time to eat brunch and ensuring we met a deadline that night. We were responsible for the livelihoods of everyone we employed, for the safety and satisfaction of our customers and for the huge capital outlays that came from trying to grow. All of that equals a lot of stress and not much sleep for a group of young entrepreneurs.

We're not proponents of girlboss culture, but we do believe there is a reality to growing an international business that can't be ignored: it is hard work. It is unrelenting. You will work nights, weekends and it will take you away from your personal life. You must decide if you want that – if you value growing something bigger than your own personal life – before you ever step foot in the ring.

After eleven years at the helm of frank body, we knew our time was coming to an end. After many months of assessment of our core values, our wants and our desires (all while juggling newborns, small children and multiple businesses), we both knew that working eighty-hour weeks was no longer aligned with the vision we had for our lives. Our life's purpose was not to sit in meetings and create spreadsheets until we died. It was to discover what life was all about. We wanted more time for exploring new ideas, hobbies, family, friends and doing work that felt more strategic and creative than what our roles had grown into. We were creative writers at the end of the day, and had found ourselves writing nothing but emails and performance reviews. We wanted to recreate lives where we actually had time to be creative and write again. But that choice was a privilege that took fifteen years to earn – stepping off the playing field isn't something most of us can do at twenty-five. We are highly ambitious people who decided our version of stepping back included growing Willow & Blake, writing a book and launching two new businesses together. It wasn't about doing less – it was about having more space to find ourselves at the beginning again. Now, in our education business For Scale, we coach founders and find ourselves wrestling with the reality of what it took to grow frank body and not wanting every founder to experience the same type of burnout we did.

So how can you get comfortable with being uncomfortable, and how do you create frameworks for sustainable growth?

Organisational Strategies for Sustainable Growth

- **INVEST IN LEARNING:** A founder who thinks they have nothing to learn is a founder who literally can't be taught. One of the best things we did was upskill. We devoured every piece of *Harvard Business Review* content out there. A podcast came out? We listened to it. We engaged a coach to help us define our leadership style and cultivate a workplace culture that we were proud of and navigate the complex elements of our best-friend/co-founder dynamic.
    - *Tip: Make sure you learn **and** implement. Listening to endless podcasts is only helpful if you actually do something with the information.*

- **SET REALISTIC EXPECTATIONS:** Understand that running a large, international business requires significant dedication, including working nights and weekends. Clocking off at 5pm to meet your friends at the pub can work, but you'll probably need to clock back on at 9pm. Alternatively, you can choose to be more intentional and create something that supports the lifestyle you want to live. Can you work four hours a day in those initial months or years? Probably not, but maybe you also don't need to work a hundred hours a week like we did.

- *Tip: No one actually notices or cares whether you log back on at night.*

- **MAKE STRATEGIC HIRING DECISIONS**: Even in periods of rapid growth, you want to expand your team slowly and carefully to avoid having to unwind hiring decisions later or bloating the staff line on the profit and loss statement so much that it costs you all of your profitability. There is a good way to grow and a bad way to grow. Trust us – we've done both.
    - *Tip: Engage a professional to help you plan your organisational chart. A mentor or coach who was a founder is ideal because they understand the realities of business.*

- **FOCUS ON CLEAR COMMUNICATION**: Clarity is kindness. Remember that. Learn to voice your feedback and opinions clearly without fear of confrontation, and maintain that approach no matter who you are talking to, from investors to leadership to new staff – everyone is valued and clarity is important. We all do better when we know what the people around us think and need.
    - *Tip: Don't wait for the perfect time to say what you're thinking or be influenced by others in the room. Have an opinion and be clear about it.*

- **EMBRACE NOT KNOWING**: Ironically, there will always be questions you can't answer or things you don't know as a founder. Foster psychological safety by admitting what you don't know and maintaining a learning mindset. You'll find that you create a team that don't hide their mistakes from you.

  - *Tip: Practise saying 'I don't know' in the mirror. Then say it to your co-founders. Then your senior staff. Then your wider team. It gets easier with time, and your business gets better because everyone develops a solutions mindset rather than relying on you to fix everything.*

- **STAY FOCUSED**: Avoid spreading resources too thin by trying to seize every opportunity. We made that mistake and it cost us. Every 'yes' means saying 'no' to something else.
  - *Tip: Most entrepreneurs are attracted to the shiny new thing. We'll hustle to complete a project, but running the day-to-day is not as fun. Make sure you have the bandwidth to execute with excellence or someone to delegate to.*

- **TRUST YOUR INSTINCTS**: While being strategic is important, don't overthink decisions – your first instinct is often correct.
  - *Tip: As crucial as it is to say you don't know, it's also important to act swiftly. Don't um and ah. Decide like your life depends on it. Choose one menial task on your list today and make a decision. Do that again tomorrow. Keep flexing the muscle and it will get strong.*

Personal Strategies for Managing Founder Stress

- **CREATE NON-NEGOTIABLE ROUTINES**: Whether it's a morning meditation, exercise, drinks with friends or walking meetings – establish daily practices that protect your mental health and stick to them religiously. Don't try to run an eight-figure business on three hours of sleep – that's a great way to run yourself into the ground.

  - *Tip: Start with a simple habit. We recommend a gratitude journal called* The Five Minute Journal. *It can change your perspective.*

- **SET BOUNDARIES WITH TECHNOLOGY**: Implement designated 'offline hours' where you're unreachable. Use this time to recharge, connect with friends or pursue hobbies outside of work. You know those things normal people do?
  - *Tip: Delete work apps like Slack from your phone to create literal boundaries with technology. There is no reason to be reachable and online twenty-four hours a day.*

- **PRACTISE MINDFUL LEADERSHIP**: Schedule regular check-ins with yourself to assess your mental state and energy levels. Be honest about when you need to step back or seek support.
  - *Tip: Investing in your mental health is non-negotiable. Counsellors or coaches can provide support on a casual or regular basis.*

- **BUILD A SUPPORT NETWORK**: Connect with other founders who understand your journey. Having peers to share experiences with can help normalise the challenges and provide practical solutions.
  - *Tip: Live by the motto 'A rising tide lifts all boats'. The founder experience is unique and having others in the same boat as you makes it feel less lonely.*

- **SCHEDULE RECOVERY TIME**: Block out regular periods for complete disconnection from the business. This might be a quarterly weekend away or an annual extended holiday.
  - *Tip: Everything will work if you unplug it for a while. Get out into nature and let your mind wander.*

- **DELEGATE EFFECTIVELY**: The worst thing we see founders do over and over is refuse to let go. Learn to trust your team and let go of tasks that don't absolutely require your attention. This creates space for strategic thinking and prevents burnout. It also creates happier teams.
    - *Tip: At some point, you are no longer the best person to do everything. Founders often try to micromanage every project and stay in the detail of every aspect of the business when they actually can't, so they hold up their team and frustrate people. Asking for 360 feedback and being willing to hear it is crucial to growing your business. Get out of your own way.*

Things Will Go Wrong

They always do. All you can do is be prepared. Let's step back to a client interaction in 2014. It was our first national client and we were working directly with the founder CEO.

His penthouse overlooked Bondi Beach. The white sand looked as though it touched the edge of his expansive balcony – Jess felt as though she could walk through the oversized glass doors and float straight into the blues of the Pacific. If we had to put a value on it, we'd say about $12 million. He was lovely and supposedly mission-driven, but he was also demanding and not that skilled in brand development – we spent a lot of time helping him keep things on the right track.

We'd flown up on our dime – which at this point in time, given the very little revenue Willow & Blake was generating in our first year of business, was a huge gamble for us – in order to tour his venues and work on the brand voice and copy rollout for them as well as the launch of another new project.

We worked tirelessly. We delivered brilliant work. That work was printed. That work was used. That work was loved. We were so proud – it was the biggest project we had taken on to date in terms of deliverables, brand exposure and budget.

A month after returning home, we followed up on our overdue invoice. There was no reply.

A few weeks later, we sent another email. He was a busy man, so we assumed it was an oversight. Again, there was no word.

After twelve months, we stopped trying and wrote off the loss in our tax return. Not only had we not been paid the project fee, but the job had in fact cost us money after we paid thousands for flights, accommodation, transit and food.

A few months later, his name appeared on the *AFR Rich List* with glowing words underpinning his name. And would you believe it when we tell you that this exact scenario happened not once, but twice within twelve months? Later that year, a different client also failed to pay their invoices, never replied to our emails and later appeared on the *AFR Rich List*. We could not believe it. But we also learned a very valuable lesson.

The moral of this story is not to tear this person down, but rather to raise your awareness of the realities of running businesses and improve your protocols for payment, in both directions.

Businesses will run into cash flow issues. It happens. And in those instances, we believe firmly in transparency and accountability. We have always held ourselves to these standards, and often, as long as people know there will be a delay, they are fairly understanding. It's when there is radio silence that things sour.

Now we have much more stringent practices and terms for payment. We want you to learn the lesson that took us years: stand up for yourself at the start. Practise the art of negotiation early. A great book for this is *Never Split the Difference* by Chris Voss, which was recommended to us by a mentor.

You Will Need to Pivot, Pivot, Pivot

Insert meme of the *Friends* characters trying to manoeuvre a couch up some stairs.

We were sitting around the boardroom in our weekly new product development meeting. We unashamedly all admitted this was our favourite meeting of the week.

This was the meeting where we got to touch, smell and test all our new products. This was where we workshopped new briefs and fine-tuned existing ones. The room was always filled with new smells, fun textures, laughter and colour.

This meeting, however, was not going to plan. The Triple Acid Body Wash had failed stability testing *again* – after eighteen months of development and ten rounds of feedback. The body wash we had sold into retailers around the world as our triple-A launch of the year had again failed stability testing. What the f. And let's be clear, that f does not stand for 'frank'.

Why did it fail? The gel structure was separating from form in the aqueous phase. We were (again) trying to do something no other brand had done before: turbocharge a body wash with active ingredients normally used in facial skincare products. Not one type of acid but three to give your skin triple the benefits.

The manufacturer's advice was to reduce the active ingredients – but that simply wasn't an option.

The repercussions for this launch were large. Our team had been working on the plans for this product and launch for over a year. The final art was done, the product was sold in and the marketing plans were ready. We'd also based our forecasts on a launch that was now looking like it needed to be pushed out indefinitely.

We faced a tough discussion. Reduce the active ingredients to make a good-but-not-great product and meet our deadlines for launch? Or reformulate the product with the current active levels in a new base, hope to pass stability testing, make a great product and subsequently push out the launch and send our marketing department into overdrive again, finding a creative way to fill the revenue gap? Option two won, as it always should.

This product hinged on efficacy, and actives were the key to that. We'd repositioned our brand as high-performance body care, moving far away from our coffee roots, and this product was a pivotal product in that new direction.

By this stage, our manufacturers had become used to our persistence, and they knew we wouldn't take feedback like this lying down. They rallied to innovate and create the formula we wanted.

Our team had also become well accustomed to the pivot, and sprang into action.

Resilience is a key trait for founders and anyone working in a growth environment. You will face decisions like this day in, day out. You need to be prepared to make hard decisions. You have to be the one to stand up for the brand time and time again.

We reformulated again. Tested again. It turned out the issue wasn't the actives, but the fragrance. We chose a new fragrance, kept our high dose of actives and launched the product as intended. It was a bestseller overnight.

It always comes back to one of the earliest lessons in this book – that if you never ask the question, the answer will always be no.

THE LESSON:

Feeling nervous is good: it means you care. Lean into the discomfort.

Chapter 19

THE FUTURE OF BRANDS AND STARTUPS

Does the world need more stuff? No. Will be it made? Yes. So, if you're going to do it, make it count. Don't add another subpar product to landfill. Don't rip off someone else's hard work. Create something that solves a problem. Be passionate about solving that problem and be passionate about your customers. Make something you're proud to tell people you built. Really, at the end of the day, the future of brands isn't that different to what it has been for the last fifty years.

What comes next? Oh, if only our crystal ball could clearly lay out the path! No one knows exactly what is in store, especially when businesses are so impacted by global factors outside of their control as the last five years have shown us: war, illness, economic and political instability will all impact your business. Change in business has never been so rapid and unexpected. We need to accept that being a founder is a constant practice in patience, surrender and agility.

What we do know is that many of the mistakes we have made over the last fifteen years are ones that will continue to be mistakes for businesses long into the future, so learn from ours. Here they are, in no particular order:

- **DON'T HIRE TOO MANY PEOPLE:** In periods of rapid growth, it's easy to get ahead of yourself, hiring people and breaking out one role into five. Yes, you need to invest in people to grow, but do it slowly and surely. There is nothing more disheartening for the founder and the team than having to unwind hiring decisions. This is not to mention the even bigger impact this has on the people in the roles you have to make redundant.

- **GET GOOD AT HIRING AND ONBOARDING:** Get a coach, do a course, learn how to ask non-leading questions. Interviewing people is an art and onboarding them properly into your organisation is crucial to set them up for success. We didn't always do this well, so we took the time to learn.

- **SAY WHAT YOU THINK:** Many people, in an effort to avoid confrontation, don't voice their opinions clearly or loudly enough. We made this mistake many times and now, twenty years into our careers, have finally learned to untangle the concepts of clarity and confrontation. They are not the same thing.

- **ADMIT WHAT YOU DON'T KNOW:** It's okay to not know everything, even if you're the boss. The biggest flex in business is to have an appetite to be always learning, to ask questions, to be okay with not knowing and seeking out the answer. Doing it in front of your team is an A+ boss move because you create an environment of psychological safety where the team feels comfortable to ask questions, take risks and make mistakes.

- **DON'T BE EVERYWHERE:** Trying to seize every opportunity and grow into every region is a dangerous game of spreading yourself and your team too thin. It's easy to run out of the money you need to support the growth properly and then you end up doing none of it well. This very problem threatened the livelihood of our business more than once. Remember: every 'yes' is a 'no' to something else.

- **YOUR PREFERENCES DON'T MATTER:** Your thoughts and feelings, if they are not part of the business strategy, are largely unimportant when it comes to making big decisions in business. Everything should come back to the strategy. If you catch yourself saying 'I think' or 'I feel', you're most likely on the wrong track.

- **YOUR FIRST INSTINCT IS USUALLY RIGHT:** As much as you need to be strategic, you also need to not overthink things. Your job is to provide direction and clarity to the team. Often, your first instinct is the right one. If you have to convince yourself an idea is right, it's probably wrong.

A chat with Connor Archbold – co-founder, Tracksuit

Tracksuit is a brand-tracking platform that we have used for years. Previously, collecting data on brand-level metrics was notoriously difficult, expensive and unreliable. As people who are often making arguments to convince CEOs and CFOs to listen to their marketing managers and invest in long-term brand building, we have found this tool vital in arming us with data that we would have otherwise had a hard time collating. We interviewed Connor Archbold, co-founder of Tracksuit and man at the helm of a brand data mountain, about what he sees for the future of brands and startups.

What trends are you seeing in the data that speak to the importance of brand building during tough economic times?

What we know is that a strong brand:

- makes customer acquisition easier and cheaper (lower CAC);
- makes existing customers buy more products more often (increases LTV);
- acts as a moat for the company against competitors and market turmoil.

The brands that hold on (or even increase) brand spend during downturns are in pole position for when a growth market kicks off again.

What role do you believe community building will play in the success of future startups, and how might this evolve?

In a world where AI is prevalent, one of the key changes we'll see as entrepreneurs is that the barrier to entry on products in any category comes down significantly. With AI, it will get easier and easier to code or produce any product and launch it into the world.

If you agree with the above statement, the key moat for any business becomes brand, loyalty, trust and community.

At Tracksuit, we believe the next generational businesses will have to have strong communities and brands (that's why we spend so much energy on it … and 'cause it's more fun).

How do you envision the balance between digital presence and physical retail changing for brands in the coming decade?

Retail and experience is an important part of brand and community. It's one of the best ways to build trust with consumers. Let them touch and feel your product, service and brand.

In the future, it will be incredibly important for brands to invest in great experiences for their customers, and this will often include a retail experience.

What emerging technologies do you think will have the biggest impact on startup operations and scalability?

What changes do you anticipate in consumer behaviour? Do you have any expectations that startups should prepare for?

This is a personal belief … but I think that the loneliness epidemic is very real and getting worse the more time we spend online and disengaged from humanity. This will impact how people live and what they look for in brands and communities.

How do you think the concept of brand loyalty will evolve in an increasingly digital and competitive marketplace?

1. Trust. Trust. Trust.
2. The better AI gets, and the easier and cheaper it is for companies to exist purely within digital/AI spaces, the more trust people will require to switch from a brand they know and love.
3. Older brands will have more trust.
4. It will be harder for new small brands to convince folks that they are high quality.
5. This is why the creator economy is booming. People trust the folks they follow and see content from every day, so it helps brands to show up in trusted digital spaces.

What skills and capabilities do you believe will be most crucial for startup founders in the next decade?

First-principles thinking and creativity will always be important. Standing out and being unique will be even more obvious, special and defensible – because everything produced by AI is inherently derivative.

What are you doing to future proof your own business?

- Building a B2B brand like a B2C brand.
- Building community by trying to solve the work problems of our ideal customer profile (ICP) whether it's related to our product or not.

- Always breaking the mould and trying to stand out. Whether it's something small and digital like a pricing page, or something big and physical like wearing a bright purple tracksuit to a black-tie investor event!

What brands do you see doing interesting things to set themselves up for future wins or category domination?

My favourite brand in the world: Paynter Jacket. Follow them. This is intentional and brilliant brand and community building. I want to buy literally anything they sell.

When we think about the future of startups, we're excited. We believe the best brands are yet to be created. The rise of technology is leading to the invention of products that simply couldn't have existed ten years ago.

There are more resources out there for people starting brands than ever before. And that means more people will be starting brands, which means better brands are coming.

But competition fuels progress.

It's not the fanciest, most complicated or the most well-funded startups that will succeed; it's the ones that best connect with an audience. The startups we're most excited about are the ones that fill a genuine need or solve a problem simply.

For us, brands and campaigns are not just logos and pretty pictures – they are reflections of society. They connect with people and can make them feel something: joy, disdain, nostalgia, indifference. Selling stuff, sure, that's part of it – but what's really special is building communities, legacies, and making something that's bigger than yourself and continues to grow even after you've left.

Every day we meet new founders and we're blown away by their creativity, tenacity and passion. One thing that continues to be clear is that there's no blueprint for what a founder is or should be, and there's no blueprint for how to build or run a business. Just because something has always been done one way doesn't mean it's the right way.

The quicker you realise everyone is making it up the better. If you're thinking about starting something and wondering when the right time is, understand that it's never the right time. Feel the fear but still make the move. And remember, you have to risk it for the biscuit.

When it's Time to Move on

You know when you're at a nightclub and the lights come on and they start blasting that Eazy-E and NWA song that tells you to 'Get the fuck out'? The remaining club goers look at each other with horror, their masks of darkness removed, and the floor is littered with empty vodka sodas. You realise you should have left hours ago and commence the walk of shame towards the exit, entering the street and feeling the brisk morning air on your skin and the harsh glow of the sun in your eyes, only to see gym goers heading towards their 5am spin class.

That's what it feels like the day you wake up and realise you need to move on from your own company.

Six months before we sat down to write this manuscript, we had one of the most difficult conversations we've ever had as founders: where do we go from here?

Willow & Blake was almost fifteen years old.

frank body was on the precipice of its eleventh birthday.

We had built hundreds of brands, collectively worth over $1 billion, and had hired, supported and waved goodbye to many employees over the years.

We'd managed one-hundred-hour work weeks while pregnant; we'd juggled demanding board meetings while breastfeeding; we'd had record sales days; appeared on TV; won awards and received the most heartfelt emails from clients and customers.

But one day, it wasn't enough anymore.

Founders are a curious breed. Like bowerbirds, we are constantly collecting ideas and we burrow them away for a future date. At some point, that date comes, and you need to decide if you can keep doing what you're doing – which is most likely managing other people doing the cool stuff you love – or if you need to hire other people in management so you can once again start building something from scratch. Because it is, after all, an itch that never ceases for almost every founder we've ever known. There's only so long you can ignore it.

Jess is a creative and brand builder at heart. She longed to be back at the start of the journey, to bring to life the myriad ideas she had but had no time to think about. It had been nagging at her for years. That feeling of longing for more time to explore new projects and be with her family was the ultimate decision-maker. For many people, change is scary. For Jess, the only thing scarier than a new idea is an old one. Change is a welcome challenge. Being at the start is the most exciting phase of all, because the essence of creativity is not what exists already, but what could exist. Finding her way back to the beginning after travelling down a long and winding path was a very worthwhile journey. Now she enters the next phase of her career – rebranding a legacy Australian brand, starting a new consumer brand, writing and growing Willow & Blake – armed with lessons she couldn't have imagined learning and a respect for the commercial aspects of a business that most creatives never get to see. She does it in a part-time capacity so she can have time with her kids each week, a juggle that is never easy but always worth it.

After her journey at frank body ended, Bree was lost. She knew she'd made the right move, but she realised that in all the podcasts and books she'd read, founders don't often talk about how strange it is to step back from a company you built. You go from being busy, having a team of people relying on you and having your identity tied to a company ... to a blank slate. There's a Milan Kundera line from *The Unbearable Lightness of Being* that Bree thinks of often: '... when nobody wakes you up in the morning, and when nobody waits for you at night, and when you can do whatever you want. What do you call it, freedom or loneliness?'

Bree worked with a coach to reframe her mindset around associating being busy with success and gave herself time to reset after fifteen years of building.

Bree didn't have to look far for her next chapter – she took over as Managing Partner at Willow & Blake. There, she gets to do what she loves: build brands, a team and a life centred around her values of creativity, autonomy, family and connection. Willow & Blake has always been an incredible business and since the founders' return (Bree full time and Jess part time) it has thrived. The team has grown, our clients' brands have grown, and the work the agency is putting out today is some of the best in the country.

The itch to start something new is hard not to scratch and the startup phase is Bree's favourite, too; the hint of an idea that becomes a reality. It's messy and chaotic, but that's where creativity thrives. So as expected, she threw herself back into the chaos – this time with a new perspective: you've done it before, you can do it again. Listen to your body not your head and choose joy.

When reflecting on how the decision to move on from our active roles in frank body – the brand we had built with our own blood, sweat and tears – aligns to our core values, it's clear that it was creativity and freedom that we both missed the most. We had spent the last seven or so years in particular management roles where the crux was spreadsheets, budgets and HR. It wasn't what we loved, despite loving our brands and the people within them. We lived in meetings, where there was seldom room for creativity and ideas due to the reality of a C-suite role.

We craved the possibility that comes at the very start of an idea. The 'what if?' and 'wow, are we really going to do this?' conversations.

Once you realise what's missing from your life, it becomes impossible to ignore. The business and brand ideas that we had tucked away in metaphorical binders for so long were now swirling around in our dreams, in our passing thoughts, and in the moments we stood in the shower or drove to the shops. We couldn't not act on them.

It wasn't an easy decision to step aside and let the next generation of leaders we had spent years training take the lead, but it was the right one.

Now here we are once again building something alongside you – writing business plans, talking with business partners, sourcing manufacturers, designing logos and websites, developing a fresh tone of voice, creating packaging and marketing strategies. We're solving a problem and filling a need; creating something cool and memorable that slots neatly into that white space you now know so much about.

Even though we're at the end of the book, the reality is that we're all at the most exciting phase of all – the beginning. From here, the only way is up.

From the ground up.

J & B x

ACKNOWLEDGEMENTS

We may have written this book and lived this life, but all of it happened with the help, ideas, creativity, tenacity and support of some very important people, who we would like to thank.

Firstly, our families. Dan, Jess's husband, and Steve, Bree's husband, who have always believed in us and supported us without question. To our children, who provide us endless joy and help keep our moral compass in check. To our parents and siblings, who packed scrub and shouted from the rooftops, even when they didn't quite understand what we were doing.

To our co-founders – Steve Rowley and Alex Boffa – and shareholders for their brilliance and support of our desire to share our story in order to help more young entrepreneurs. To our teams, past and present, at Willow & Blake and frank body, who put their blood (not literally), sweat and tears (literally) into building these companies with us. To our clients, who have trusted us to work in partnership with them, building their brands from the ground up.

To our wonderful publishing team: Kelly Doust (publisher), Genevieve Day (agent), Zoe Sorenson and Kevin O'Brien (project editors), Sam van

Zweden (copyeditor), Lucy Bell (proofreader), Alissa Dinallo (cover designer), Nashin Mahee (production), Kasi Collins (publicist) and Alistair Trapnell (marketing).

And, perhaps most importantly, to each other. For twenty years of friendship. For sixteen years of business. For all the highs, lows and moments in between. Here's to the next twenty.

REFERENCES

1 Kim, W. Chan and Renée Mauborgne , *Blue Ocean Strategy*, Harvard Business Review Press, 2004, 2015.

2 Grede, Emma, *The Founder Playbook* podcast, 'How Michael Rubin Built Fanatics by Betting on Obsession', 13 May 2025, podcasts.apple.com/nz/podcast/the-founder-playbook-how-michael-rubin-built-fanatics/id1811878340?i=1000708288260.

3 Rand, Paul, *Design, Form, and Chaos*, as cited in Heller, Steven, *AIGA Journal of Graphic Design*, Vol. 3, No. 4, 1995.

4 Nicholls, Charles, 'The Customer Acquisition Crisis', simplicitydx.com, 2024, simplicitydx.com/blogs/customer-acquisition-crisis.

5 Dubin, Michael, 'DollarShaveClub.com – Our Blades Are F***ing Great', YouTube, uploaded by Dollar Shave Club, 7 Mar 2012, youtube.com/watch?v=ZUG9qYTJMsI&ab_channel=DollarShaveClubeClub.

6 Valinsky, Jordan, 'Casper's IPO Is Officially a Disaster', cnn.com, 5 Feb 2020, cnn.com/2020/02/05/investing/casper-ipo-share-price/index.html.

7 Bomey, Nathan, 'Working from Home, in Your Bed? You're Not Alone. Mattress Sales Are Soaring during the Pandemic', usatoday.com, 12 Oct 2020, usatoday.com/story/money/2020/10/12/mattresses-adjustable-basescoronavirus-pandemic/5900740002.

8 Holder, Sarah, 'What's the Future of the "Sleep Economy"?', bloomberg.com, 23 Jan 2020, bloomberg.com/news/articles/2020-01-22/online-mattress-seller-casper-bets-big-on-stores.

9 Trainer, David, 'Don't Buy Casper, the Latest Money-Losing IPO', forbes.com, 5 Feb 2020, forbes.com/sites/greatspeculations/2020/02/05/dont-buy-casper-the-latest-money-losing-ipo.

10 LeSavage, Halie, 'Casper, Bed in a Box Pioneer, Makes a Lackluster Stock Exchange Debut', retailbrew.com, 8 Feb 2020, retailbrew.com/stories/2020/02/07/

casper-bed-box-pioneer-makes-lackluster-stock-exchange-debut?utm_campaign=mb&utm_medium=newsletter&utm.

11 Statistics on the impact of brand building from McKinsey & Company (mckinsey.com), Harvard Business Review(hbr.org), Nielsen Brand Impact Studies (nielsen.com).

12 Hartnett, Nicole, 'Ehrenberg-Bass Q&A: What Happens When Brands Stop Advertising?', Ehrenberg-Bass Institute, Adelaide University, 2022, marketingscience.info/news-and-insights/ehrenberg-bass-qa-what-happens-when-brands-stop-advertising.

13 Crimtan, 'Why Brands Need to Keep Advertising in Tough Economic Times – According to 100 Years of Data', crimtan.com, 3 Jan 2024, crimtan.com/why-brands-need-to-keep-advertising-in-tough-economic-times-according-to-100-years-of-data.

14 Branding Strategy Insider, 'Recession Marketing Success Requires Boldness', 20 April 2009, https://brandingstrategyinsider.com/recession-marketing-success-requires-boldness/#:~:text=Over%20the%20years%20hundreds%20of,companies%20that%20advertised%20the%20most.

15 MarketSense study, as cited by Hamner, Susanna, 'Double Down on Strategic Advertising', cbsnews.com, 17 August 2010, cbsnews.com/news/double-down-on-strategic-advertising.

16 Deveau, Richelle, Sonia Joseph Griffin and Steve Reis, 'AI-powered Marketing and Sales Reach New Heights with Generative AI', McKinsey & Company, 11 May 2023, mckinsey.com/capabilities/growth-marketing-and-sales/our-insights/ai-powered-marketing-and-sales-reach-new-heights-with-generative-ai.

17 Bain & Company, 'Customer Behavior and Loyalty in Banking: Global Edition 2023', March 2023, https://www.bain.com/insights/customer-behavior-and-loyalty-in-banking-global-edition-2023/.

18 Deloitte Digital, 'Personalizing Growth', 11 June 2024, deloittedigital.com/us/en/insights/research/personalizing-growth.html.

19 Nielsen, Nielsen Digital Ad Ratings and Annual Marketing Report 2024, nielsen.com, 2024, nielsen.com/insights/2024/maximizing-roi-in-a-fragmented-world-nielsen-annual-marketing-report/?utm_source=press&utm_medium=press-release&utm_campaign=2024-report-annual-marketing_nlsn_global&utm_content=annual-marketing-report__press-release_04-25-2024.

20 Google Marketing Platform Study by Dervişoğlu, Yonca, 'Top Digital Marketing Trends and Predictions for 2023', November 2023, business.google.com/us/think/consumer-insights/digital-marketing-trends-2023.

21 Hootsuite, Hootsuite Social Media Trends Report, 'The Top Social Media Trends for 2026', hootsuite.com, 2026, hootsuite.com/research/social-trends?utm_campaign=all-tier_1_campaigns-social_trends_2024-glo-none-------&utm_source=press_release&utm_medium=corporate_communications&utm_content=

22 *Harvard Business Review Magazine*, 'How Brands and Influencers Can Make the Most of the Relationship', May–June 2023, https://hbr.org/2023/05/how-brands-and-influencers-can-make-the-most-of-the-relationship.

23 Interbrand, 'Best Global Brands 2024', interbrand.com, 2024, interbrand.com/best-global-brands.

24 Husson, Thomas, '2024 B2C Marketing Priorities and Challenges', forrester.com, 31 May 2024, forrester.com/blogs/2024-b2c-marketing-priorities-and-challenges.

25 PwC, 'PwC's Global Crisis and Resilience Survey 2023', pwc.com, 30 Mar 2023, pwc.com/gx/en/issues/crisis-solutions/global-crisis-survey.html.

26 Foss, Alexander, et. al., 'LinkedIn Workplace Learning Report 2024', LinkedIn.com, 2024, learning.linkedin.com/content/dam/me/business/en-us/amp/learning-solutions/images/wlr-2024/LinkedIn-Workplace-Learning-Report-2024.pdf.

27 Staplehurst, Graham, '10 Key Takeaways: Kantar BrandZ Most Valuable Global Brands 2024', kantar.com, 5 Aug 2024, kantar.com/north-america/inspiration/brands/10-key-takeaways-kantar-brandz-most-valuable-global-brands-2024.

28 Kapferer, Jean-Noël and Vincent Bastien, 'The Luxury Strategy: Break the Rules of Marketing to Build Luxury Brands', The Rabbit Hole, Blas Moros, https://blas.com/luxury-strategy/.

29 Elle Girl Japan, 'Ariana Grande: Elle Girl Japan Interview [JAPANESE SUBS] (8/29/2014)', YouTube, uploaded by AriAnastasia Grande, 1 Aug 2024, youtube.com/watch?v=-dgnZ0XG-pU.

30 Aesop Chief Customer Officer Suzanne Santos, as quoted in Sams, Lauren, 'How Aesop Turned into a Billion-Dollar Brand', afr.com, 23 Feb 2023, afr.com/life-and-luxury/fashion-and-style/how-aesop-quietly-turned-culthandsoap-into-a-billion-dollar-brand-20221215-p5c6m8.

31 Parents at Work and UNICEF Australia, 'National Working Families Report 2024', parentsatwork.com.au, 2024, members.workfamilyhub.com.au/national-working-families-report-2024.

32 Workplace Gender Equality Agency Australia, 'Advancing Paid Parental Leave and Flexibility in the Workplace', wgea.gov.au, 8 Nov 2024, wgea.gov.au/flexible-work/advancing-gender-equitable-take-up-of-ppl-and-flexible-work.